Vegan Family Style

MY VEGGIE JOURNEY

KASHA LINDLEY

FriesenPress

Suite 300 - 990 Fort St
Victoria, BC, V8V 3K2
Canada

www.friesenpress.com

Copyright © 2021 by Kasha Lindley
First Edition — 2021

Edited by Kim Lindley
Photographs by Kendra Perkinson

To my Best friends Laura and Racheal for always being there to support me in anything I set my mind to.
To My sister who helped out with my surgeries and my husbands deployment so I could concentrate on my family and writing this book.
To my in laws who are always there for me when I needed them most.
To my mom who started me on this journey and never gave up on me.
And to my husband, the love of my life, who is my number one fan and my biggest supporter.

ISBN
978-1-5255-9203-4 (Hardcover)
978-1-5255-9202-7 (Paperback)
978-1-5255-9204-1 (eBook)

1. COOKING, VEGETARIAN & VEGAN

Distributed to the trade by The Ingram Book Company

This very amazing gal has some amazing vegan recipes and is always asking to try new recipes that you may know! This gal has a heart of gold!! Keep up your veggie journey!! Your doing amazing!!
—SHELBY HERBERT

Great Recipes and fun to follow, there's always something new and different to try.
—MISSY BELL

So knowledgeable and inspiring, Coming up on a year in November being plant based pescatarian. I have learned so much!! Keep doing what you are doing!!
—TARA BROWN

She's real, she knows the best way to describe and lead people in the right direction to her best abilities in sharing vegan recipes.
—TAM MARSHALL

Love the simplicity of the recipes. Easy to find ingredients. Makes it so much easier to stay on this journey of better Health.
—CHRISTINA NAVARRO HOWERTON

This is my journey on health, nutrition and wellness. I'm excited to share my love and passion for cooking delicious, nutritious, plant-based meals, as well as what I've learned about foods that reduce inflammation based on the effects it can have on your health and well-being. I am a stay at home mom of four beautiful children and wife to an amazing husband in the Air Force. My life can be pretty busy, but I'm always pushing myself to do better for my family. As a former ballet dancer/teacher I strive to be healthy by cooking wholesome, nutritious meals. I have a 10-plus years medical history with chronic pain due to fibromyalgia, persistent pain in my chest and arms caused by thoracic outlet syndrome (TOS), as well as protruding discs in my neck, spinal stenosis and spinal spondylolisthesis in my back. It can make everyday tasks difficult, such as vacuuming, laundry, cleaning and yes, even cooking. I push through these struggles, because I truly believe changing my lifestyle to a plant-based diet can relieve some, if not all of my pain. I have tried several diets, from the Mediterranean diet to the Keto diet and none have alleviated my pain, in fact, some even made them worse! In January 2019, my husband and I made a New Year's resolution not to eat meat for a whole year. I started to research meat-less recipes. I took a "Forks over Knives" course through the Rouxbe College of Culinary Arts in March of 2019 and loved every minute of it. I also completed this year their "Professional Plant-Based Cooking Course." I started creating my own recipes, which led me to start a Facebook page where I shared these recipes weekly on my site called "My Veggie Journey." I found that eliminating meat and dairy from my diet has helped me tremendously, not only to lose weight, but to keep my inflammation & pain under control. It has made such a difference in how we feel, after that year my family decided to make this our way of life! So, my friends, I'm going to show you some easy steps how to transition your life into a more vegan friendly way of living. I'm truly grateful for this opportunity and I hope this helps you and your family find your way to a more healthy, *Vegan Family Style* life.

CARBS ARE NOT YOUR ENEMY!

Carbs have been given a bad rap, when in fact they are an essential part of our diet. There is a big difference between good carbs and bad carbs. Don't compare a donut to a potato because one is a highly processed food, while the other is a whole nutritious vegetable. It's when you combine animal fats (butter, sour cream) and too much processed sugar that it becomes unhealthy. The highly processed food combined with the carb is the number one reason for inflammatory issues as well as weight gain. One of my favorite meals is a baked potato with mashed avocado and roasted veggies. Carbs are essential for kids as well. They crave starchy foods because their bodies and muscles are constantly growing. My kids love to eat my homemade french-fries, just baked in the oven. As long as you are meeting your daily caloric needs, there is no need to track protein intake or use protein supplements with plant-based diets. The longest-lived people on Earth, the Japanese, get about 10% of their calories from protein, compared with the U.S. average of 15-20%. They have rice for every single meal and they are considered the healthiest people on the planet because they live on such a low processed food diet, based on whole foods, high carbs and lots of veggies. Look up "The China Study" The Most Comprehensive Study of Nutrition Ever Conducted and the Startling Implications for Diet, Weight Loss and Long-term Health is a book by Dr. T. Colin Campbell and his son, Thomas M. Campbell II.

VEGETABLE VS. MEAT DIGESTION TIME

Diets higher in fiber are associated with faster digestive time. Because plant-based foods make up a greater part of the vegetarian diet, vegetarians consume more fiber than meat-eaters, therefore, food moves through your intestines at a more rapid rate. The Canadian Society of Intestinal Research says that vegetarians tend to have faster bowel transit times and more frequent bowel movements than omnivores. The difference in transit times can be attributed to the amount of fiber in the diet. Bacteria that live in your gut prefer carbohydrates found in fiber. Whenever there are less carbohydrates to consume, food takes longer to pass through the colon and harmful bacteria are produced because the bacteria start to feed on leftover protein instead. According to the USDA Dietary Reference Intake Table, you need 25 to 30 grams of fiber daily. Any less, may cause slower transit times, especially with the digestion of meat in the human digestive system. Meats contain higher amounts of fats than fruits, vegetables and grains. Fats takes more time, effort and extra specific enzymes to be broken down and digested which tend to slow digestion.

TIPS

READ YOUR LABELS FRIENDS! If you could make just ONE change towards health, it should be ditch ARTIFICIAL FAKE SWEETENERS. These sweeteners become instant gut toxin and neuro (brain) toxin. Sucralose is often hidden in protein powders, most chewing gum, sodas, energy drinks. Aspartame is in many processed foods too! Check out all the symptoms and diseases they are connected to.

Also drinking lots of water and green tea during the day helps with weight loss.

Some of you are ready to transition to vegetarian immediately. But if you're like most people, it's hard to go totally meatless overnight. You've probably got a freezer full of meat that you paid good money for. My advice to you is to start out slow and steady, like the tortoise and the hare. Slow and steady wins the race every single time. Start out with meatless Mondays and then maybe try going meatless three days a week. Next, you might try to eat meat only on the weekends, and so on until you feel comfortable with cooking a vegetarian diet. Then, do the same to transition with from vegetarian to vegan. Start out with one day out of the week going completely egg and dairy-free. Week by week, you will find it is easier and easier not to exclude animal products in your daily meals. Remember, we all work at a different pace so don't judge yourself too harshly when you slip up. Just pick yourself back up and keep moving forward and never give up on becoming a healthier you! My kids are more vegetarian than they are vegan which is fine by me. I give them choices and let them learn to make healthy decisions for themselves, but I continually put healthy and nutritious fruits, vegetables and carbs out for them. Kids love to learn, so make it fun while being educational. Learning how food is made, especially if they can grow it themselves, is a great way to entice children to learn to love their veggies. Also, talk about how vegetables help the different parts of your body; walnuts are good for your brain health, tomatoes are good for your heart, leafy greens are good for blood flow and so on. My goal is that one day, they will grow up and have good, nutritional eating habits.

Duration of Digestion: Meat Diet vs. Vegetarian Diet

By Adam Dave Updated November 9, 2018

Reviewed by Sylvie Tremblay, MSc

Pantry

Like most of you, I'm on a budget, so I plan my menu by what's on sale. Just as you did with meat, you want to look at the fruits and veggies on sale in your grocery store and make your menu by what is available. Don't be afraid to substitute when my recipes have something you can't find. If all else fails make it yourself at home, such as sour cream.

BREAKFAST

Egg substitutes for baking

Applesauce

Mashed banana

1 Tbsp flaxseed with 2 Tbsp water

JUST egg

Bob Mills egg replacer

Produce

Bananas, oranges, apples, berries & avocados (if they're on sale, I buy them unripe and leave them next to my bananas and when they are ripe, I place them right away in the fridge where the eggs go), potatoes of all kinds.

I like buying avocados super ripe as well, I peel & cut them up and put them in the freezer for smoothies and ice cream. I do the same thing with spinach when it's on sale, pop it in the freezer! Both should be good for three to six months.

Pantry

Steel cut oats, nuts (any kind - walnuts are usually the cheapest) My favorite go to thing is making a large amount of steal cut oats on Sunday night and keeping them in the fridge so I can grab and go as much as I want. I love using mashed banana in the bottom of the bowl then add your oatmeal cinnamon and blueberries with a little plant-based milk and your good to go.

dried fruits like apricots, dates, cherries, raisins

multi grain bread (I use Dave's killer bread) but really anything multi grain is good.

Peanut butter or almond butter.

Chia seeds

Freezer

Any kinds of fruit that is on sale (Strawberries are usually the cheapest in the freezer section).

When bananas start going bad, I peel them and put them in the freezer to use in smoothies or ice cream later. I also but my vegan yogurt in the big pints so it's cheaper and you get more for your buck.

Produce

Potatoes of any kind, I like baking a whole bunch of potatoes, keeping them in the tin foil, putting them in the fridge and saving them for lunch. Potatoes are cheap!!!

Salad stuff, I buy romaine lettuce in bulk and chop it up and put it into Ziploc baggies. Roma tomatoes, cucumbers, peppers, baby carrots and celery.

Hummus is a must have for sandwiches, Buddha bowls and dipping your veggies.

Pantry

Beans of any kind, black beans, navy beans, garbanzo beans.

You're going to be putting them in your salads from now on. If you don't like beans you can always use brown rice and nuts.

Salsas of any kind. Dressings like balsamic vinaigrette. Potatoes are your "go to" friend. Buy a huge bag, wrap them in foil and bake them all at the same time. Put them in the fridge when they are cool for easy on-the-go lunches. Pair it with your favorite veggies and dressings or mashed avocado and salsa, and your good to go.

Freezer

I fill my freezer to the brim with broccoli, green beans, corn, brussel sprouts and spinach. These are going to be your toppings for your baked potatoes. Buy the cheapest kind, it doesn't have to be organic!!

Fridge

Celery, carrots, onions and garlic.

Peppers, broccoli and cauliflower.

Any other veggies that might be on sale. Don't go for the ones that you think you might use, look for the ones that you know you're going to use. Plus, if corn is on sale stock up on corn!!

Tofu, mushrooms and Tempeh if you can find it. Vegan cheese can be expensive so I don't buy it very often. If you can't find vegan cheese, I have some great recipes on how to make it.

Potatoes again!! I don't buy the already pre-cut french fries because 1) they are way more expensive than a bag of potatoes and they don't last as long. 2) they usually have additives we don't need.

Making your own fries is easy and cheap, just cut them into wedges, use salt, pepper, paprika and olive oil and separate them out on a cookie sheet and bake at 400° for 30 minutes. Instant, cheap and good for you!!

Pantry

Protein pastas, like chick pea pasta, soybean pasta, and black bean pasta.

Marinara sauces, (no Alfredo) brown rice and quinoa.

More beans. Lol!! Beans are cheaper than beef, so it's easy on the pocket book.

Olives, artichokes and pickles

Flour, of your choice I like using King Arthur flour because it is a higher in protein flour.

Veggie broth, I make my own from my veggie scraps. I put all my scraps in a Ziplock baggie in the freezer and when it's full I add salt and pepper to a big pot of water and boil it down for about 1 hour, put them into mason jars or you can freeze them in containers.

Freezer

Same as lunch. I also look for veggie burgers and nuggets. Remember The grocery store can sometimes be your biggest nightmare because of just how much it costs. They have it set up for you for spend as much money as you can on junk food that doesn't last long or fill you up. Labels are misleading and just because something says "Low fat" or "sugar free" usually stands for chemical laden and weight gain. If you shop with the mindset of "how can I spend as little as I can" vs "I need to buy everything I need" you will find its easier than you think. Also remember that whatever money you were spending on meat and dairy before now goes to your new plant-based budget. We are a family of 6 and we usually spend anywhere from $600 to $800 a month on food at the grocery store. We also don't eat out a lot because it's usually too expensive.

CONDIMENTS AND SPICES

Spices & condiments go a long way in making your dish beautiful and enhancing the flavor. Don't be afraid to try out new spices. Smoked paprika, chili powder, onion powder, garlic powder, curry powder, cumin, cayenne pepper, ginger, red pepper flakes, dried thyme, dried basil, dried parsley, dried oregano, dried rosemary, cinnamon, bay leaves, are just to name a few. But if I was stuck on an island with only one spice to take with me it would have to be herb de Provence.

Make sure and have all kinds of different vinegars like red wine vinegar or white wine vinegar, vegan Worcestershire sauce, balsamic vinegar, apple cider vinegar and regular vinegar. These are going to add flavors to your sauces and dishes. It would be good to also have all kinds of different cooking wines like Marsala wine, red wine, white wine, sherry wine. As far as oils go, grapeseed oil, olive oil, coconut oil are the only oils that I use.

Peanut butter, Almond butter, Tahini sauce and vegan yogurts, (I buy these in the tubs because they are cheaper.)

Agave nectar, brown sugar, and sugar in the raw as well as maple syrup and stevia are my go-to sweeteners for all of my baking dishes.

Keep your usual baking needs such as baking powder baking soda vanilla extract cornstarch but add to it flaxseed meal and chia seeds as well as nutritional yeast.

EATING OUT

This is probably the hardest thing to do being plant-based and even harder for kids because menus for kids are designed for picky eaters. We don't stick to a strict no meat rule when it comes to eating out with the kids because there are fewer options for them. As for me and my husband, we order meals like veggie fajitas without the cheese and sour cream. However, more and more restaurants are offering vegan and vegetarian options, which is great. Always remember to ask, "Is there any dairy, eggs or chicken and beef stock in it." My stomach cannot handle beef anymore since I've changed to this lifestyle. I ordered pho one time without the meat forgetting that the broth was still made with the bones and I paid for it all night long. Also, McDonalds fries are not vegan, I made that mistake too. When in doubt call ahead and ask what their options are. Below is a list of some fast food options:

Subway – Veggie delight with all the veggies and guac, even kid's meals can be done this way

Burger king – Impossible burger and fries (Yes, they are not fried in animal fat). Also, their French toast sticks

Taco bell – This is my number one favorite place!! Because they can make anything on their menu vegan

Papa Johns – Usually get a large pizza extra sauce and all the veggies and breadsticks

Chipotle – Need I say more, Build your own vegan burrito

Wendy's – Baked potatoes!!

Panera – Mediterranean salad and sandwich, just ask for no cheese. Also, their Baja grain bowl, again with no cheese.

Panda Express – Chow Mein with tofu and eggplant, also veggie fried rice for the kids

Donut shop – Beyond beef breakfast sausage sandwich without cheese and any of their coffees with almond milk

Baskin Robbins – yes you can still take your kids out for ice cream because they make non-dairy options.

AVANLEA'S BREAKFAST MAG PIES!!

Avanlea and I made these about a year ago and we've been making them ever since. They are a great breakfast item for kids, and they freeze well too!!

4 cups gluten-free oats

½ cup wheat germ

2 cups plant-based milk

1 cup maple syrup

1 cup applesauce

2 bananas

1 cup peanut butter

Flax and chia seed egg (4 Tbsp water and 1 Tbsp each flaxseed and chia seed)

1 Tbsp baking soda

2 tsp cinnamon

1 tsp salt

Chocolate chips, berries, or nuts for toppings.

Mash the bananas then place the rest of the ingredients in the bowl, mix, scoop into muffin tins or use a bread loaf pan. Use any toppings that you like (Chocolate chips, nuts, berries etc.). Bake in the oven at 350° for 20 minutes for muffins, or 1 hour for the loaf pan.

BANANA PEEL BACON

Not going to lie, I know it seems crazy but all I can say is you have to try it before you judge it!!

- **6 ripe banana peels, deveined**
- **½ cup soy sauce**
- **¼ cup maple syrup**
- **1 tsp smoked paprika**
- **1 tsp onion powder**
- **1 tsp garlic powder**
- **½ tsp liquid smoke**

Combine all of your ingredients except for banana peels and mix until well combined. Take the back of a butter knife and scrape the remaining veins from the inside of the peel. Once you have removed all the veins from the banana peel, soak in the marinade for at least 20 minutes.

In a medium size pan add enough olive oil until about one inch in the pan. Heat on medium-high, then one at a time, add the banana peel to the hot oil and cook on both sides for 1 minute each. They cook really quickly so try not to burn them. Place them on a plate with paper towels and let them dry.

PB&J PANCAKES

This is my husband's favorite all-time pancake recipe; it was the first thing I made him when he got back from deployment.

- 2 cups flour
- ½ cup brown sugar
- 1 tsp baking soda
- 2 Tbsp baking powder
- ½ cup rolled oats
- 1 Tbsp cornmeal
- 1 Tbsp flax seeds
- 1 tsp cinnamon
- 1 tsp salt
- 2 tsp sesame seeds
- 1 cup applesauce
- 1 cup almond milk
- ½ cup water
- ½ cup plant-based butter melted and cooled at room temperature

In a medium bowl whisk together all of your dry ingredients until well combined. In a smaller bowl add applesauce and the rest of your liquid ingredients. Mix until well combined. Slowly add the liquid ingredients to the dry ingredients. On a medium high skillet add your batter ½ cup at a time. Cook for 2 minutes on each side. Add your favorite almond butter, jam and sliced bananas on top!! So good!! Enjoy!!

XANDER'S BLUEBERRY SWEET POTATO PANCAKES

My kids love, love, love, blueberries so of course I had to make them some yummy blueberry pancakes.

1 cup sweet potatoes, mashed

1 cup flour

1 cup oats

1 Tbsp baking powder

1 Tbsp sunflower oil

1 Tbsp flaxseed

1 Tbsp chia seeds

3 Tbsp maple syrup

½ tsp salt

½ cup blueberries

2 ½ cups almond milk

Mash sweet potatoes and add the rest of the wet ingredients to a medium sized mixing bowl stirring until all combined. Then add your dry ingredients to a smaller bowl and whisk together. Slowly add the dry ingredients to your wet ingredients until well combined. In a sauté pan On a medium high add ½ cup of batter at a time. Cook for 2 minutes on each side. Enjoy!!

MORNING GRANOLA

So good and so healthy!! It's great to add to your yogurt or atop your favorite smoothie bowl. It's also a great cereal for your kids!! You can add any of your favorite ingredients and nuts or fruits. Make it your own. I love topping this on my morning yogurt for an on-the-go option.

6 cups rolled oats

2 cups wheat germ

1 cup sunflower seeds

½ cup pecans, chopped

1 cup pumpkin seeds

1 cup maple syrup

½ cup agave nectar

½ of olive oil

1 tsp vanilla extract

1 tsp cinnamon

Mix all of your wet ingredients in a small bowl and set aside. Mix all of your dry ingredients in a large bowl and add wet ingredients, mixing well. Then place on two baking sheets lined with parchment paper split the granola and half and spread evenly. Place in a 300° oven for 20 minutes. This stores great in a mason jar or in a freezer bag. Enjoy!!

VEGAN MEXICAN BREAKFAST BURRITOS

My husband is a huge fan of breakfast burritos, so naturally I had to make these for him.

1 bag of beefless crumbles or tofurky chorizo plant-based crumbles

1 onion, chopped

2 Tbsp garlic

1 Tbsp chili powder

1 tsp paprika

1 tsp cumin

1 tsp oregano

1 bottle of JUST egg

1 bag of spinach

12 whole wheat tortillas

Salsa of your choice

In a medium sized cast iron skillet, sauté onions in olive oil until translucent and add garlic. Cook a few more minutes then add all your spices and beefless crumbles. Add salt and pepper to taste. In another skillet drizzle olive oil and add spinach, sauté until wilted and add salt and pepper to taste. Place in a small bowl and set aside. In the same pan drizzle olive oil and add the JUST egg, continue to cook like scrambled eggs and add salt and pepper to taste.

To assemble, place two tortillas down overlapping each other and start with the beefless crumble mixture, the add eggs and spinach. Top with dairy-free pepper jack cheese and salsa. Fold in the sides and roll into a burrito. Place burrito on parchment paper and roll again and place in a Ziplock gallon size bag and put in the freezer. To reheat, place in the microwave on high for two and a half minutes. Enjoy!!

HOMEMADE BREAD IN A BAG

The kids love making bread in a bag, it was actually a homeschool project that I did with a group of homeschoolers down in Biloxi, MS that I co-led. We met on Tuesday mournings and I would teach a cooking class once a month. This recipe was a big hit. My kids will make this on the weekends for breakfast.

1 gallon-sized Ziplock bag

3 cups all purpose flour

2 Tbsp of agave necter

1 Tbsp of rapid rise yeast

3 Tbsp of olive oil

1 cup warm water

1 tsp salt

Place 1 cup flour, yeast, salt, agave necter, and oil in the bag. Seal tightly and let the kids mash it til its well combined. Then take the remaining flour and one cup at a time seal the bag and mash again until the dough is pulling apart from the bag. Then place on the countertop and knead for about 5 minutes. Then separate out into two separete loaves and place them into two bread pans and let rise for about and hour. In a 350° oven place your loaves in for about 20 to 30 minutes. Enjoy with my vegan butter and homemade jam!!

VEGAN "BUTTER" AND PEACH JAM

Made homemade bread yesterday with vegan butter and homemade peach jam!! Southern comfort food at its finest!!!

Vegan Butter:

- 1 can of full-fat coconut milk, just the top layer, not the water underneath. (I put mine in the fridge overnight to separate)

- 1/3 cup coconut oil

- 1 Tbsp apple cider vinegar

- ½ tsp salt

- 2 Tbsp sunflower oil

- 1 Tbsp nutritional yeast

Heat milk, coconut oil and apple cider vinegar in the microwave for a minute and a half. Then add to a blender with salt, sunflower oil and nutritional yeast and blend for a minute. Put in a container and refrigerate for 24 hours then it's ready to spread on toast!!!

Peach jam:

- 2 lbs. of peaches, diced

- 1 cup maple syrup

- 2 Tbsp chia seeds

- 1 Tbsp cinnamon

- 1 tsp nutmeg

Place all ingredients in a large saucepan on medium high heat for about 30 minutes to 1 hour. Stirring occasionally to ensure maximum thickness then add to any size mason jars you have and label.

SMOKED TOFU SANDWICHES

There is a food truck in Downtown Omaha that has a fantastic Tofu Sandwich and I was inspired by their creation and my hubby's pellet grill/smoker.

1 pkg of Extra Firm Tofu (pressed for 24 hours, frozen for 6 hours then pressed again for another 24 hours) This step is crucial for getting a wonderfully dense texture.

½ cup soy sauce

1 tsp liquid smoke

1 tsp smoked paprika

1 tsp garlic powder

1 tsp onion powder

¼ cup maple syrup

Once the tofu is fully pressed, slice it into long strips and place in the bottom of a medium sized dish. In a small bowl add the rest of your ingredients and mix together until well combined. Add the liquid ingredients on top of your tofu and marinate for 6 hours. When ready, place your tofu on your smoker which should be set at 240° and let cook for 45 minutes. Put this on any sandwich to complete your lunch. This is a wonderful way to replace turkey sandwiches!!! Enjoy!

ARABELLA'S TOMATO SOUP WITH GRILLED CHEESE SANDWICHES

My sweet Bella-boo came up with this recipe all on her own and I couldn't be more proud!!

Tomato Soup:

   4 cans of diced tomatoes

   1 medium sized onion, diced

   4 stalks of celery, diced

   1 Tbsp garlic

   1 handful of basil, chopped

   1 handful of parsley, chopped

   2 tsp dried thyme

   2-8 oz cans of Veggie broth

   1 cup red wine

   1 Tbsp red wine vinegar

   2 Tbsp olive oil

   Salt and pepper to taste

In a large stock pot on medium-high heat add olive oil, onion, salt and pepper. Cook until caramelized. Add celery and cook for a few more minutes. Add garlic and dried thyme and cook a few more minutes then add wine and red wine vinegar. Once the vinegar has evaporated add tomatoes veggie broth and cook for 30 more minutes. Put it in a blender and blend until smooth. Return back to the pot and add your basil and parsley.

Cheese Sandwich:

- 1 cup cashews
- ¼ cup nutritional yeast
- 2 Tbsp olive oil
- 2 tsp arrowroot powder
- 1 Tbsp cornstarch
- 1 tsp garlic powder
- 1 tsp onion powder
- 1 tsp smoked paprika
- ¼ tsp turmeric
- 1 tsp salt and pepper, each
- 1 tsp maple syrup
- 1 Tbsp lemon juice
- 1 Tbsp apple cider vinegar
- 1 ½ cups veggie broth
- 1 Tbsp lemon juice

Soak the cashews in boiling water for 15 minutes. Drain and transfer the cashews to the container of a blender. Add the remaining ingredients and blend until smooth. Pour the mixture in a saucepan, then bring to a boil over medium-high heat, stirring constantly. When the mixture reaches the boiling point, keep simmering for 2 minutes, then remove from the heat. Pour the mixture into ramekins. Cover with plastic wrap and refrigerate for at least 2 hours or overnight.

Once set, spread on whole grain bread. Put a small amount of vegan butter on the bottom of the pan on medium high heat. Grill sandwiches on both sides until golden brown. Serve with soup and enjoy!!!

EGGLESS EGG SALAD SANDWICH

Not going to lie, I was skeptical about using tofu when I first started this lifestyle, but I am a huge fan now because of this recipe!!

Egg salad:

1 pkg of tofu pressed for 30 minutes.

1 stalk of celery, chopped

1 carrot, diced

1 tsp turmeric

1 tsp paprika

1 tsp onion powder

1 tsp garlic powder

2 Tbsp green onions

1 Tbsp Dijon mustard

1 recipe for avocado mayo (see below)

2 Tbsp nutritional yeast

Black Salt and pepper to taste (Trust me it's worth getting, found it on Amazon)

Break apart and mash the tofu then Mix together the rest of your ingredients and serve on whole grain bread, top with lettuce, tomato, and avocado.

Avocado Mayo:

- 1 ripe avocado
- 2 Tbsp white wine vinegar
- ½ of a lemon, juiced
- 1 tsp garlic powder
- 1 tsp onion powder
- 4 to 6 Tbsp plant-based milk
- Salt and pepper to taste

Blend all ingredients in a blender until smooth, use on your favorite sandwiches.

SHIITAKE SUSHI

For those of you missing sushi right now this is not only a tasty recipe but fun to make as well.

Sushi rice:

- 1 cup glutinous sweet rice
- 2 cups water
- 1 Tbsp rice wine vinegar

Place all ingredients in your Instapot and put on high for 12 minutes or just press the rice button.

Mushroom marinade:

- ½ cup soy sauce
- ¼ cup maple syrup
- 1 tsp paprika
- 1 tsp onion powder
- 1 tsp garlic powder
- ½ tsp liquid smoke

Mix all ingredients in a small bowl and set aside.

- Nori sheets or seaweed sheets
- Carrots, shredded
- English cucumbers, sliced thinly
- Baby Bella mushrooms, sliced thinly
- Avocados, sliced thinly
- Sushi rice (above)

Evenly dip sliced mushrooms in marinade and set aside on a plate. To assemble, place nori sheets on a bamboo sushi maker. add about a ½ cup rice and using warm water in a small bowl, dip your fingers and spread the rice out evenly. Then in the center of the sushi roll add a bed of shredded carrots, English cucumbers, sliced mushrooms, and avocado. Fold in half and with the bamboo sushi maker squeeze tightly then fold and squeeze tightly again. Slice with a serrated knife and dip in your favorite dipping sauce. Enjoy!!

KALE SALAD WITH ROASTED RADISHES AND QUINOA AND BROWN RICE

I hated radishes growing up but I never thought to roast them in the oven. My favorite go-to for any veggie is to roast it because it helps bring out the sweetness.

Kale Salad:

- 1 bunch of kale
- Cherry tomatoes
- Radishes for garnish
- 1 avocado
- The juice of half a lemon
- Salt and pepper to taste

Chop up the kale and place in a medium sized bowl. Squeeze out the avocado from the rind (No need to dirty a spoon) and mash it together with your hands. This is a great job for your kids to do. Then add your other ingredients and mix until well combined.

Roasted Radishes:

- 2 bags of radishes
- 2 Tbsp olive oil
- 2 tsp dried thyme
- Salt and pepper to taste

Cut the ends off of the radishes then cut them in half. Place them on a cookie sheet lined with parchment paper. Drizzle with olive oil then add dried thyme, salt and pepper to taste. Put into a 400° oven for 20 minutes. Enjoy!!

THE ULTIMATE PB&J SANDWICH

National Peanut Butter and Jelly Day!! My girls and I dressed up as our favorite Disney princess and built a fort and made the ultimate PB&J sandwich, complete with homemade berry jam and almond butter!! Since I didn't have peanuts, I used almonds instead.

Almond Butter:

- **3 cups unroasted dry almonds**
- **3 Tbsp agave nectar**
- **1 tsp salt**
- **1 tsp almond extract**
- **Water, add as needed**

On a cookie sheet add almonds and place in a 400° oven for 10 to 15 minutes. Let cool completely before you begin. Add all of your ingredients to a food processor and blender for 10 to 15 minutes. Add water, a Tbsp at a time until you get a smooth consistency.

Berry Jam:

- **2 cups mixed berries, (raspberries, blueberries, blackberries)**
- **½ cup maple syrup**
- **3 Tbsp chia seeds**
- **1 tsp vanilla extract**

Add all of your ingredients to a saucepan and heat on medium low heat for 15 to 20 minutes. Then add to your favorite jam jar. If you wish to can it run it through on the highest setting of the dishwasher to can and store for later. Let it run all the way through. Or enjoy right away!!

GRANDMOTHERS FRIED GREEN TOMATO SANDWICH

Straight from the garden; fried green tomato sandwich with banana peel bacon, spinach, kale and vegan mayo!!! Best BLT I've ever had!!!

Fried Green Tomatoes:

- 4 large or 6 small green tomatoes, sliced
- 1 cup plant-based milk
- 3 Tbsp vegan mayo
- 1 cup whole wheat bread crumbs
- 1 cup flour
- 1 tsp paprika
- 1 tsp garlic powder
- 1 tsp onion powder
- 1 tsp salt and pepper, each
- 1 cup sunflower oil

In three separate dishes, separate out plant-based milk, flour and bread crumbs. Add vegan mayo to milk and whisk until combined. Add paprika, garlic powder, onion powder, salt and pepper to flour mixture whisk to combine. Take a slice of green tomatoes, dip in milk mixture, then dip in flour mixture and back into the milk mixture. Roll in bread crumbs. Add sunflower oil to the pan and heat on high. Cook green tomatoes for 2 to 4 minutes on each side and lay on paper towels to dry.

Use your favorite whole wheat bread, vegan mayo and add your ingredients on top of each other. Enjoy!!

CHILI CHEESE FRIES

I had a huge hankering for chili cheese fries so I made it vegan of course!!

French fries:

- 4 russet potatoes, sliced lengthwise
- 1 Tbsp salt
- 3 tsp paprika
- 2 tsp black pepper
- 3 Tbsp olive oil

Place the sliced fries in a medium sized bowl. Then add olive oil and salt pepper and paprika. Place fries evenly on a cookie sheet and Place in a 400° oven for 30 to 40 minutes until nice and golden brown.

Chili Sauce:

- 1 lbs. of mushrooms, minced
- 1 cup walnuts, chopped
- 1 small onion, chopped
- 1 Tbsp garlic
- 1 Tbsp tomato paste
- 1 cup veggie broth
- ½ cup tomato sauce
- 1 Tbsp vegan Worcestershire sauce
- 1 tsp liquid smoke
- 1 Tbsp chili powder

- 1 tsp paprika
- ½ tsp cayenne pepper
- 1 tsp garlic powder
- 1 tsp onion powder
- 1 tsp oregano

In a cast iron skillet, add a tablespoon olive oil and sauté onion and garlic. Once onion starts to caramelize, place mushrooms in pan and continue to cook down for 5 minutes. Add vegan Worcestershire sauce, liquid smoke, tomato paste and continue to cook for another 2 minutes.

Add all of your spices and your veggie broth. Cook another 5 minutes then add tomato sauce. Once everything is combined add walnuts.

Easy vegan Cheese sauce:

- 1 large Yukon gold potato
- 2 large carrots
- ¼ cup nutritional yeast
- 1 Tbsp apple cider vinegar
- 1 tsp salt
- 2 Tbsp olive oil
- 1 tsp turmeric
- 1 tsp garlic powder
- 1 tsp onion powder
- 1 cup veggie broth

Boil potato and carrots until fork tender, about 20 minutes. Then place all ingredients in the blender and blend until smooth. Best served warm. Can also be used as a base for Mac and Cheese.

Place fries on the bottom of your dish then add your chili and cheese sauces, enjoy!!

DAD'S APPROVED PORTOBELLO MUSHROOM BURGER

Made portobello mushroom burgers with garlic and paprika French fries!! My dad, who's a big beef eater even loved it!!!

- 2 portobello mushrooms, scraped and cleaned of gills.
- ¼ balsamic vinegar
- ¼ cup soy sauce
- 2 Tbsp vegan Worcestershire sauce
- 1 tsp garlic powder
- 1 tsp onion powder
- 1 tsp liquid smoke
- 1 tsp paprika
- 2 Tbsp maple syrup

In a medium-sized bowl, add all of your ingredients, mixing well. Soak your mushrooms in the marinade for 30 minutes, flipping halfway through. Grill on a grill for 5 minutes on each side. Add your favorite burger toppings and enjoy!! Goes great with prosecco onion rings.

GRILLED CAESAR SALAD

Grilled Caesar salad is an absolutely amazing new way to enjoy your salads!! I'm not a salad girl but I was in the mood one night so I came up with this and it was the bomb!!

Dressing:

¼ cup tahini

The zest and juice of half a lemon

2 tsp capers

1 tsp Dijon mustard

1 tsp white wine vinegar

2 garlic gloves

2 Tbsp olive oil

¼ cup water

Salt and pepper to taste

Salad:

½ head of romaine lettuce

Cherrie tomatoes

And breadcrumbs

Put everything except for lettuce in a blender and blend until smooth. Cut a small romaine lettuce in half and grill on the grill for a few minutes on each side; long enough to get a char on it. Then place upside down on a plate and add tomatoes, cucumbers, peppers and breadcrumbs. Top with the dressing. You can also add chicken-less grilled chicken, Enjoy!!

MEDITERRANEAN BLACK BEAN TAPENADE

A lunch that was inspired by the middle eastern naan bread and Mediterranean olive and black bean tapenade with sautéed veggies!!

Sautéed veggies:

  1 zucchini, diced

  1 yellow squash, diced

  1 tomato, diced

  1 red onion, diced

  6 mushrooms, sliced

  1 Tbsp garlic, minced

  2 Tbsp red wine vinegar

  1 tsp herb de Provence

  Salt and pepper to taste

Sauté onions until caramelized then add mushrooms and cook down for about 5 minutes. Add red wine vinegar and cook down for a few more minutes. Add the rest of your vegetables and herbs de Provence, salt and pepper and cook for about 5 more minutes until veggies are tender.

Olive and black bean tapenade:

  1 can of black beans, rinsed

  1 cup mixed olives such as green olives and kalamata olives and their juices

  ½ red onion, diced

  2 garlic cloves

  ¼ cup olive oil

The juice of half a lemon

1 handful of parsley

Salt and pepper to taste

Blend everything together in a blender until smooth.

Naan bread:

2 ½ cups flour

5 oz plain plant-based milk yogurt

1 cup warm water

2 Tbsp olive oil

1 Tbsp active dry yeast

1 Tbsp agave nectar

1 tsp salt

Mix everything together in a small medium bowl. Then take dough and set aside for 10 to 15 minutes. Sprinkle flour on a countertop and one handful at a time roll out the dough until a quarter of an inch thick. Then in a medium sized iron skillet add olive oil till about an inch from the pan and heat on medium high heat. Cook naan bread on both sides for about 1 to 2 minutes each.

CHICKPEA SALAD SANDWICH

Growing up my mom and Nana always made the best chicken salad sandwiches, so here's my version of it, Lunch is served!!

1 can of chickpeas

3 Tbsp vegan mayo

½ red onion, chopped

1 Tbsp dill

1 tsp onion powder

1 tsp garlic powder

1 Tbsp agave nectar

1 Tbsp Dijon mustard

¼ cup sunflower seeds

½ cup green apple, chopped

½ cup cranberries

The juice of half a lemon

Salt and pepper to taste

Combine all ingredients in a bowl, mashing chickpeas as you stir. I use Dave's killer bread with 21 whole grains and seeds, add two slices of tomato, lettuce and avocado!! Boom!! Killer sandwich!! Enjoy!!

PROSECCO ONION RINGS

This was actually created by accident; I was really intending to use a beer batter but unfortunately, I did not have any beer so prosecco was the next best thing!! And yes, I ended up drinking the other half of the bottle while eating these onion rings!!

2 large onions, sliced into 1 inch slices

1 cup gluten-free flour

1 cup prosecco (AKA Italian beer)

1 tsp paprika

1 tsp garlic

1 tsp onion powder

Salt and pepper to taste

Oil for frying

Place all ingredients except for onions and oil in a bowl and mix until well combined. Heat the oil in a frying pan to 375 degrees. Take a slice of onion and dip in the batter and place in hot oil. Cook on each side for 2 minutes. Place on a paper towel and salt to taste. Goes great with portabella mushroom burgers. Enjoy!

MY SISSY POOH'S EGGPLANT BLT

I can't take credit for this; my sister had this brilliant idea and I'm so glad she did!! Eggplant BLT!!!

1 Eggplant, cut into thin strips

¼ cup soy sauce

1/8 cup maple syrup

1 tsp paprika

1 tsp garlic powder

1 tsp onion powder

1 Tbsp vegan Worcestershire sauce

Whisk all ingredients in a bowl and set aside. Slice eggplant into thin strips and line a baking sheet. Soak the eggplant in the marinade on each side, then lay on baking sheet. Bake in the oven for 30 to 45 minutes at 300° until crispy. Use your favorite slices of bread and vegan mayo, top with tomatoes and lettuce and enjoy!!!

KID-FRIENDLY ZUCCHINI FRITTERS

My mother-in-law sent me this recipe and told me to try it with the kids so that's exactly what we did!! I made an easy pizza sauce to go with it!!

Zucchini fritters:

1 cup breadcrumbs (I make my own from the heels of the bread leftover. Just dice them up, and toast them in the oven at 350 ° for 10 mins and pulse them in the food processor. Keep in a mason jar.)

¼ cup nutritional yeast

1/3 cup chickpea flour

2 cups shredded zucchini (squeeze the excess water out in a dish towel)

2 flax seed eggs (two Tbsp flaxseed and 4 Tbsp water mixed together and set aside)

½ cup plant-based milk

1 tsp garlic powder

1 tsp onion powder

1 tsp smoked paprika

1 tsp salt and pepper, each

¼ cup oil for frying (high heat oil like sunflower, avocado)

Mix everything together except for oil in a large mixing bowl until well combined. Using about half of a cup of batter, flatten into small thin pancake fritters and set aside on a plate. In a cast iron skillet, add your oil on medium-high heat and fry for a couple of minutes on each side. Set aside on paper towels to dry.

Pizza sauce:

- 1 small onion, diced
- 1 Tbsp garlic
- 1 can of tomato paste
- 1 ½ cups water or veggie broth
- 1 Tbsp oregano
- 1 tsp salt and pepper
- 1 handful of fresh basil
- 1 handful of fresh parsley

Using the same cast iron skillet, sauté your onion and garlic until caramelized. Add your oregano and cook for another minute, then add your tomato paste and slowly add your water. Cook for about 5 to 10 minutes. Sprinkle with your basil, parsley, salt and pepper. Enjoy!!

FAMILY BURRITO BOWLS WITH CILANTRO LIME SAUCE

We had a wonderful friend invite us over for dinner one night and she made this amazing cilantro sauce for our burrito bowls and it was a major hit in our house!!

Burrito Bowls:

Cooked Brown rice

Cooked sweet potatoes

Black beans

Corn

Mashed avocado

Salsa

Vegan sour cream

Cilantro lime sauce:

1 big handful of cilantro

The juice of 2 limes

1 tsp garlic powder

1 tsp onion powder

1 tsp cumin

1 tsp smoked paprika

¼ cup water

2 Tbsp olive oil

Salt and pepper to taste

Blend everything in a blender until well combined. Enjoy!

VEGAN CARBONARA

I think my favorite all-time pasta has to be this one, not only because I had to think way outside of the box to replace both the egg and bacon but because the flavor is out of this world!!!

Cream sauce:

- 1 cup cashews soaked overnight
- 1 cup macadamia milk
- 2 Tbsp nutritional yeast
- 1 Tbsp white wine vinegar
- 1 tsp turmeric
- 1 tsp garlic powder
- 1 tsp onion powder
- Salt and pepper to taste

In a blender, blend everything together until smooth. Set aside.

Sauce and spaghetti:

- 1 onion diced
- 1 bunch of asparagus, cut into 1-inch
- 1 cup peas
- 1 cup cooking wine
- 1 Tbsp chopped up sun-dried tomatoes
- 1 pkg of spaghetti
- Salt and pepper to taste

In a large pot, bring water to boil adding 2 Tbsp salt. Cook pasta until Al dente about 8 to 10 minutes. In a medium-sized saucepan add 2 Tbsp vegan butter and 1 Tbsp olive oil. Add onions and cook until caramelized. Add asparagus, peas, and sun-dried tomatoes. Add cooking wine and continue to cook down for another few minutes. Add the cashew cream sauce to the pan and heat through for about 5 minutes. Once noodles are cooked add them to the pasta sauce and stir until well combined. Finely chop up your banana peel bacon and add vegan parmesan and parsley for garnish. Enjoy!!

AANG'S CHICKEN-LESS CHICKEN STIR FRY

My family and I love having Japanese nights at our house. We love watching a new anime and eating Asian cuisine. Our favorite is "The last Airbender."

One pkg of tofu pressed for 24 hours, then put in the freezer for 6 to 12 hours. Thaw and press again for another 12 hours. (This is essential to achieve firmness in texture)

½ cup soy sauce

¼ cup maple syrup

4 Tbsp rice wine vinegar

2 Tbsp sesame oil

¼ cup sunflower oil or grapeseed oil

2 Tbsp garlic

1 Tbsp ginger, minced or powdered

Cornstarch slurry (¼ cup cornstarch ½ cup veggie broth)

1 bunch of broccoli, chopped

4 carrots, sliced

1 onion, chopped

Mix all the ingredients for marinade in a small bowl, in a separate bowl tear apart tofu into bite sized pieces then add marinade. Set in the fridge for 30 minutes. Then Place tofu one at a time in a searing hot pan and cook on each side for a few minutes each. Take tofu out of the pan then add little more oil and your onion and begin to sauté. Once onion starts to caramelize add carrots and broccoli. In a separate bowl add veggie broth and cornstarch and mix until well combined. Then add the rest of your marinade to the veggie stir-fry and the cornstarch slurry. Cook down for about 5 minutes then add your tofu and cook a few more minutes. I make sticky rice on the side for a side dish. Enjoy!!!

MEXICAN STREET CORN AND POBLANO SOUP

Me and my Tex-Mex background just had to come up with a killer poblano soup!!

Two poblanos roasted in the oven at 500° for 10 to 15 minutes set aside and let cool. When completely cooled, peel off the skin and remove the stem. If you wish, remove the seeds but I keep the seeds for extra bit of spiciness. Dice and set aside.

Poblano soup:

4 ears of corn, remove the kernels but keep the stocks

6 cups veggie stock

2 cups water

1 large white onion, chopped

2 russet potatoes, peeled and chopped

4 cloves of garlic, minced

6 stalks of celery, diced

2 Tbsp vegan butter

2 Tbsp olive oil

2 tsp smoked paprika

2 tsp cumin

2 tsp chili powder

1 Tbsp Mexican oregano

Salt and pepper to taste

1 lime juiced

Chopped Cilantro and vegan sour cream for garnish

In a large stock pot or Instapot on medium-high heat add butter and olive oil and onion and start to reduce down until onion is nice and caramelized. Then add your garlic, celery, potatoes and all of your spices. Cook down for another 5 minutes then add your corn, poblanos, and corn stalks as well as veggie stock and water. Cook on high for 20 to 30 minutes until potatoes are nice and soft. Remove corn stalks, and add half of the soup mix to a blender and blend until smooth then add back into the pot and cook for another 5 minutes then turn off the heat. Serve with homemade tortillas and garnish with cilantro and Tofutti sour cream!! Enjoy!!

GRILLED ZUCCHINI LASAGNA

I'm a huge lasagna fan and when I have the time, I love making the noodles from scratch. It's by far one of my favorite dishes.

Cashew cheese:

1½ cups cashews, soaked overnight or boiled on the stove for 10 minutes

1 tsp onion powder

1 tsp salt

2 Tbsp nutritional yeast

½ cup veggie broth or water

The juice of half a lemon

1 Tbsp apple cider vinegar

1 garlic clove

Black pepper to taste

Blend everything together in a high speed blender and it's ready to use.

Lasagna:

Fresh lasagna noodles or boxed, whichever you prefer

2 zucchinis, thin-sliced long ways

3 Tbsp sun-dried tomatoes, diced

Cashew ricotta cheese

1 jar of tomato sauce

Fresh parsley and basil for garnish

First salt and pepper zucchini liberally and olive oil on both sides and grill for 2 to 5 minutes on each side. To assemble, spread half a cup of marinara sauce on the bottom of a large casserole dish. Add lasagna noodles until it covers the bottom, then add grilled zucchini. Add 1 Tbsp sun-dried tomatoes and one third of the cashew ricotta cheese. Add another layer of lasagna noodles, marinara sauce, zucchini, sun dried tomatoes, then ricotta cheese. Continue layering until everything is used. Top with basil and parsley and place in a 400° oven for 20 minutes. Enjoy!!

AUTHENTIC POLISH PIEROGIS MADE VEGAN

Being from a Polish family, I have been making these since I could sit up on my Nana's kitchen counter. So, this recipe is very near and dear to my heart; one I'm most proud of. There was a whole lot of trial and error, but I can finally say these are vegan approved and they taste amazing!! Pair with my cucumber salad or borsht soup.

Farmer's cheese filling:

1 cup raw cashews soaked overnight

½ cup vegan sour cream

2 Tbsp nutritional yeast

1 Tbsp white wine vinegar

½ cup macadamia milk

1 tsp salt

1 tsp pepper

Once cashews have soaked overnight, drain and rinse well. Put in blender and add the rest of the ingredients and blend well. Add to a strainer lined with a cheesecloth and set aside for 24 hours on the counter.

Potato filling:

4 to 6 russet potatoes, chopped

½ of the cheese filling from above

Salt and pepper to taste

Peel and chop potatoes, boil until tender and drain. With a hand mixer, whip the potatoes. Once the potatoes are beaten to a silky-smooth texture, set in the fridge to chill for 4 to 6 hours. Take out and add your cheese mixture, salt and pepper to taste and chill again for another 6 hours.

Pierogi dough:

- ½ cup vegan sour cream
- 2 cups flour
- ½ cup water
- 1 tsp salt

Mix together until well combined and dough is formed. Cut into fourths and set aside in a dish towel covered so it doesn't dry out. Roll dough out until fourth of an inch thick Then take a large drinking glass and cut out rounds for the pierogi.

To assemble:

Take one of your dough rounds and add 1 ½ tsp of potato filling, fold in half and pinch firmly around. Then and add 4 grooves to make it look like a little sun. Continue making until all of the filling has been used. In a large pot fill with water and bring to a rolling boiling, add six pierogis at a time and cook for 5 to 6 minutes until they start floating to the top. With a slotted spoon place in a colander and let them drain for a couple of minutes. While waiting, take parchment paper or wax paper to several cookie sheets and lay each of the pierogis out one at a time. every 20 to 30 minutes flip perogies so that each side gets completely dried. You can fry them up with onions and butter or freeze them in gallon-size freezer bags. Enjoy!!

GRANDMA GIGI'S BORSHT SOUP

Being a Polish mama, I take a lot of pride in trying to veganize these dishes that are close to my heart. This is my take on a Polish borscht soup!!

6 to 8 beats, peeled and chopped

4 stalks of celery, chopped

1 large red onion, chopped

1 Tbsp garlic

1 Tbsp vegan Worcestershire sauce

1 Tbsp red wine vinegar

¼ cup pickled beet juice

1 tsp allspice

1 tsp dill

1 tsp salt and pepper each

8 cups veggie broth

In an instant pot on sauté mode, add olive oil, chopped onion, salt and pepper and cook for 5 minutes. Add garlic, celery, vegan Worcestershire sauce, red wine vinegar, beet juice and cook for another 5 minutes. Add beats, veggie broth, spices and place the lid on the pot. Pressure cook for 45 minutes. Top with vegan sour cream and fresh dill. Enjoy!!

HOMEMADE PASTA

Homemade pasta taste so much better than boxed pasta!! It is by far my favorite thing to make but it is definitely a labor of love. Most pasta recipes include flour and egg and salt, but here's a good recipe that is vegan.

3 cups flour

1 cup warm water

1 tsp salt

2 Tbsp olive oil

In an upright mixer add flour and salt. In a small bowl add water and olive oil and mix well then Add to flour mixture. Mix on the first setting with dough hook for 10 to 15 minutes until dough is smooth and pliable. Take your KitchenAid pasta roller, turn on setting one. Cut dough into fourths and use ¼ at a time. Start to roll dough and fold in half each time x4. Then go to the next setting to on the roller and roll through x2. Continue until you get all the way to setting four. Go through twice and then lay out on the counter and dust with flour evenly on both sides. Then switch out for either the spaghetti cutter or the fettuccine cutter. Make sure and separate out the noodles immediately and dust with more flour otherwise they will stick together. In a large pot, fill with water and bring to a rolling boil. Add a handful of salt, You want it to taste like the ocean, and add your pasta. Fresh pasta Cooks a lot faster than boxed pasta. No more than 5 minutes, or until the pasta begins to float on top of the water. Once pasta is drained make sure and add olive oil immediately otherwise it will stick together. You can eat it as is or add your favorite sauce also goes great with my ratatouille recipe!! Enjoy!!

JACKFRUIT POT ROAST

My daughter helped make jackfruit pot roast, and it turned out amazing!! Went nicely with our bread in a bag we made.

2-14 oz cans of young jackfruit

1 bag of baby carrots

8 baby red potatoes

6 stalks of celery

1 lbs. of white button mushrooms

1 Tbsp garlic

1 onion, chopped

1 cup red cooking wine

1 Tbsp vegan Worcestershire sauce

1 tsp liquid smoke

1 Tbsp rosemary

2 tsp thyme

2 cups veggie broth

2 Tbsp cornstarch

Salt and pepper to taste

In a medium-sized pan on medium-high heat add onion and start to cook down for a few minutes, then add garlic. Drain the jackfruit and rip the pieces in half into bite-size pieces. Then add to the pan with Rosemary and thyme and cook for five minutes. then add cooking wine vegan Worcestershire sauce and liquid smoke and salt and pepper to taste.

in a small bowl on the side mixed together veggie broth and cornstarch. Then add to the pan and cook for another 5 minutes. Add all of other veggies to a cooking casserole dish, then add the jackfruit on top and cover with lid or tin foil. Place into a 400° oven 40 to 50 minutes. Enjoy!!

KID APPROVED MAC AND "CHEESE"

The Kid Approved Vegan mac and cheese that made history the other day!! So good!! Must try!! You won't be able to stop eating it!!

Topping:

- 2 Tbsp plant-based butter
- 1 cup breadcrumbs

In a medium-sized pan on medium-high heat add butter and wait until completely melted to add breadcrumbs. Toast for a few minutes and then place in a bowl and set aside.

Filling:

- 1 small onion, diced
- 3 garlic cloves, minced
- 2 Tbsp plant-based butter
- Salt to taste

In the same pan that you did the breadcrumbs in, add butter, onions, garlic and salt. Cook for 5 to 10 minutes until caramelized.

Sauce:

- 1 cup raw cashews soaked overnight or cooked on the stove for 10 minutes
- 1 cup baby carrots
- 1 large potato peeled and diced
- 1 cup plant-based milk
- ½ cup white cooking wine
- ½ cup nutritional yeast
- 1 tsp garlic powder
- 1 tsp onion powder
- ½ tsp salt
- Black pepper to taste

Take a large pot and add water and bring to boil. Add your carrots, potato and cashews and cook until fork tender, then drain. Place all of your ingredients in a blender and blend until smooth.

Pasta:

- 2 cups elbow pasta
- 8 qts of water
- 4 Tbsp salt for water

Bring water to a rolling boiling then add salt and pasta and cook for 5 to 10 minutes until Al dente.

To assemble:

Add pasta to a large bowl then add the filling and sauce and mix well. Pour into a large baking dish, spreading evenly then sprinkle with bread crumbs on top. Place in a 350° oven for 20 minutes. Enjoy!!!

MIDDLE EASTERN CURRY WITH NAAN

Last night's dinner was a huge success!! In honor of my husband's birthday and because he is deployed overseas, I did a middle eastern curry over couscous and made my own naan bread!! I'm going to be honest with you I was not a curry fan before this but now I will totally put this on the dinner list from here on out.

3 large eggplant

1 onion, diced

1 Tbsp garlic, minced

1 Tbsp ginger, minced

½ tsp red pepper flakes

1 can of chickpeas, rinsed and drained

1 whole roasted red bell pepper, chopped

1 Tbsp sweet curry spice

1 Tbsp cumin seeds

1 can of full fat coconut milk

2 cups veggie broth

A handful of cilantro

3 Tbsp Olive oil

salt and pepper to taste

In a large baking sheet, add all three eggplant and two Tbsp olive oil, salt and pepper and roast in the oven at 350° for 45 minutes. Take large pan start on medium-high heat and add one Tbsp olive oil and the onion and begin to sweat. Then add ginger, garlic, red pepper flakes and cook a few more minutes. Add cumin seeds and curry spice and red bell pepper and cook down a few more minutes then add veggie broth. Reduce heat and cook down for ten minutes. Take eggplant out of the oven and take two forks and peel the skin open and scoop out the flesh into a bowl. Add all the eggplant to the pan and mix until well combined. Then add coconut milk and turn off the heat and add cilantro for garnish. Scoop on top of your favorite rice or couscous. Enjoy!!

MERRY AND PIPPIN'S MUSHROOM STEW

Watching all "The Lord of the Rings" movies puts me in the mood for a good stew!! My inner nerd told me to make a meal for my four halflings to truly appreciate the movies even more!!

1 lb. mushroom both white button and baby Bella, chopped in half

4 large carrots, chopped

4 stalks of celery, chopped

1 cup lentils

6 russet potatoes, chopped (Samwise Gamgee approves)

1 large onion, minced

4 cloves of garlic, minced

1 bay leaf

2 sprigs of rosemary, chopped

4 sprigs of thyme, chopped

2 cans of diced tomatoes

8 cups veggie broth

2 Tbsp olive oil

Salt and pepper to taste

In a large cast-iron pot on medium high heat add olive oil and onion and cook down for 5 minutes until golden brown. Add garlic, herbs, salt and pepper and cook another few minutes. Add carrots, celery, potatoes, mushrooms, diced tomato and veggie broth. Cook over medium heat for 45 minutes until veggies are tender. Serve with lembas bread (vegan biscuits) and beer!!

LEMBAS BREAD (VEGAN BISCUITS)

1 stick of plant-based butter, softened

2 cups flour

1 tsp salt

1 Tbsp baking powder

1 tsp baking soda

1 cup cold plant-based milk

The juice of ½ a lemon

1 Tbsp lemon zest

In a medium sized bowl make sure the butter is room temperature (softened) before adding the flour. With a fork, mash together the softened butter and flour until it resembles a dry oatmeal. Add salt, baking soda and baking powder; then slowly incorporate the cold plant-based milk. After those ingredients have come together, add the remaining juice and zest from your lemon. The final product will be a soft and pliable dough. Roll the dough until ½" thick. Using a pizza cutter, make into a square and separate into equal sized rectangles. Use the pizza cutter to place an indention going from one corner to another. Place the rectangle-shaped dough onto a baking sheet and bake at 375° for 10-15 minutes or until golden brown.

TEXAN APPROVED "STEAK"

Steak:

- 1 can chickpeas
- ½ can tomato paste
- 1 Tbsp vegan Worcestershire sauce
- 1 tsp liquid smoke
- 2 Tbsp soy sauce
- 1 Tbsp red wine vinegar
- 1 Tbsp Dijon mustard
- ½ cup veggie broth
- 2 tsp smoked paprika
- 1 ½ cups wheat gluten
- ¼ cup nutritional yeast
- 1 tsp garlic powder
- 1 tsp onion powder
- 1 tsp smoked paprika
- 1 Tbsp steak seasoning
- Salt and pepper to taste

In a food processor, place all of the ingredients except for wheat gluten and process until smooth. Then in a separate bowl add ½ cup at a time of wheat gluten and the contents of the food processor and mix well. Dough will start to form and become like Play-Doh. Kneed well for 15 minutes. Then cut into 4 portions and wrap in foil. Bring a double boiler to a rolling boil and place wrapped meat in basket and steam for 20 minutes.

Marinade:

- ¼ cup soy sauce
- ¼ cup balsamic vinegar
- 1 Tbsp vegan Worcestershire sauce
- 1 tsp liquid smoke
- 1 tsp smoked paprika
- 1 tsp onion powder
- 1 tsp garlic powder
- 1 Tbsp Dijon mustard
- 2 Tbsp maple syrup

Place all ingredients in a flat dish and whisk together until well combined. Add your steaks and let set in marinade for 20 minutes, flipping halfway in-between. Grill steaks on the grill for 10 to 15 minutes until well chard. Take leftover marinade and place in a saucepan on medium high heat for 20 minutes until reduced down to half. Drizzle on top of your sliced steaks and Enjoy!!

GOKU'S VEGAN PHO BROTH

Of course, I had to include a dragon ball z meal because its mine and my husband's favorite anime to watch.

Step one:

1 bag of frozen veggie scraps

(Carrots, celery, onion, peppers, bok choy)

6 bulbs of garlic, peeled

1 stalk of lemongrass

The juice of one whole lime

The juice of one whole orange

1 bulb of ginger

1 pound of shiitake mushrooms

2 cinnamon sticks

2 tsp whole cloves

2 tsp coriander seeds

3 to 4 PODS of star anise

1 Tbsp black peppercorns

16 cups water

Place everything in a large stock pot and leave it on medium high heat boiling for 2 hours.

In a pressure cooker pressure cook for 45 minutes. Strain in a colander and large bowl.

Step two:

  ½ cup soy sauce

  ¼ cup vegetarian oyster sauce

  4 Tbsp rice wine vinegar

  4 Tbsp sesame oil

Return broth to stock pot on the stove and bring to a medium-high heat. Add in your soy sauce, oyster sauce, rice wine vinegar, and sesame oil. And reduce heat to low for 30 minutes.

Step 3:

  Cooked rice noodles

  Chopped cilantro

  Lime wedges

  Sriracha Sauce

  Sliced Radishes

  Shredded carrots

  Sugar Snap Peas

  Bean Sprouts

  Chopped Bok Choy

  Corn

  Shiitake Mushrooms

  And any other veggies you want!

Place rice noodles on the bottom of the bowl and then line up your veggies the way you want them. Scooping hot broth on top of the noodles can sprinkle with cilantro, radishes, sriracha, and lime wedge. Enjoy!!!

GLUTEN-FREE PINEAPPLE FRIED RICE

Made this the other night for the kiddos; pineapple fried rice and hot tea. Gluten-free too because I made it with quinoa!

1 cup fresh pineapple

2 cups cooked quinoa

1 onion, sliced

1 bell pepper, diced

1 cup corn frozen or canned

1 cup edamame

1 Tbsp garlic

1 Tbsp fresh ginger

½ cup soy sauce

1 Tbsp sesame oil

2 Tbsp rice wine vinegar

In a sauté pan add sesame oil and onion and cook until caramelized. Add bell pepper, frozen corn and edamame and cook another few minutes. Add quinoa, soy sauce, rice wine vinegar, ginger, and garlic and continue to cook for another 5 minutes. Turn off the heat and add your pineapple. I took the pineapple and used it as a boat. Enjoy!!

VEGAN MOZZARELLA "CHEESE"

If you can't find vegan cheese or it's just too expensive then try making it instead.

Cheese starter mix:

- 4 cups plant-based milk

- 2 pkgs of yogurt starter in powder form

- 1 ½ cups raw cashews soaked overnight or boiled on the stove for 10 to 15 minutes.

- 2 tsp xanthan gum

Blend all ingredients in a blender and set aside in a container with a loose towel over it for 12 to 16 hours.

To finish cheese:

- 1 cup tapioca starch

- 1 cup coconut oil, melted

- 1 Tbsp nutritional yeast

- 2 tsp salt

- 2 Tbsp white wine vinegar

- 2 Tbsp arrowroot powder

- One big bowl of salted ice water

Blend in the blender with your cheese starter and place in a large skillet over high heat and heat for 5 minutes until cheese becomes stretchy like taffy. Take off the heat and with an ice cream scoop, start to scoop out mixture into the ice water bath. Leave in the water bath for 30 minutes then remove and pat dry with paper towels. Use it to make a caprese salad or on your favorite pizza!! Enjoy!!

MARGHERITA PIZZA

I got to try out my mozzarella cheese this beautiful margherita pizza!! One of my favorite things to do with the kids is to have a make your own pizza night. Making your own pizza dough can be easy, simple and cheap!

Pizza dough:

1 Tbsp rapid rise yeast

1 cup warm water

1 tsp salt

2 cups flour

1 Tbsp olive oil

Place yeast and water in a medium bowl and stir. Leave it for 15 to 20 minutes until yeast is activated and bubbled. Add salt, flour and olive oil. Mix until well combined. Knead dough for 10 minutes then leave on top of the oven for 30 minutes. Turn oven on at 400 °.

To assemble the pizza:

4 Roma tomatoes, sliced

Homemade vegan mozzarella cheese

½ cup fresh basil

Olive oil for the base

3 Tbsp freshly chopped garlic

Salt and pepper to taste

Roll out the dough and place on a pan then layer with olive oil rub generously with garlic. Place the tomatoes and mozzarella cheese around the pizza dough then add a little more olive oil on top and salt and pepper. Bake in the oven for 20 to 30 minutes at 400°and then top with fresh basil. Enjoy!!!

VEGAN BRIE "CHEESE"

This I made with my mother-in-law in mind, because who doesn't love a glass of wine and a cheese board.

Cheese starter:

1 ½ cups-soaked cashews overnight or you can boil them on the stove for 10 to 15 minutes until soft.

1 cup plant-based milk

1 Tbsp nutritional yeast

1 Tbsp salt

½ cup plain nondairy yogurt

Blend all of the ingredients together in a blender and place in a plastic container with a towel over it for 12 to 16 hours. Do not refrigerate it.

To finish the cheese:

2 Tbsp tapioca starch

1 tsp xanthan gum

1 tsp garlic powder

1 tsp onion powder

1 tsp Italian seasoning

Whisk all ingredients in your cheese starter and bring it to the stove in a medium-sized pan over high heat. Continue to whisk cheese over the stove for 5 to 10 minutes until cheese starts to become stretchy. Quickly pour your cheese sauce into a round cake pan lined with an old towel or a cheesecloth. Set aside on the counter for another 12 to 16 hours.

When ready to eat, you can either spread it on a bagel or use crackers and grapes on a cheese board. Try it with raspberry preserves on top. Enjoy!!!

MOM'S QUICK AND EASY TEXAS SALSA

My mom was the best mom ever because she would make us homemade salsa every summer and we ate the crap out of it every time. This is my version of her recipe.

8 Roma tomatoes, halved

1 can of diced tomatoes

1 large onion, quartered

3 jalapenos, halved

6 cloves of garlic

A handful of cilantro

2 tsp cumin

2 tsp paprika

2 tsp chili powder

2 tsp garlic powder

2 tsp onion powder

¼ tsp cayenne pepper

Slice the tomatoes, and jalapenos in half, peel and quarter the onions. Place on a baking sheet with olive oil salt and pepper. Roast at 400 ° in the oven for 20 to 30 minutes. Place all ingredients in a blender and blend until smooth. Enjoy!!

MEDITERRANEAN LASAGNA

My mom is gluten-free so I did this recipe in honor of her, and it's easier than making regular lasagna!!

1 grilled eggplant, sliced lengthwise

1 grilled zucchini, sliced lengthwise

1 grilled yellow squash, sliced lengthwise

2 cups cooked quinoa

½ cup finely chopped marinated artichokes

¼ cup sun-dried tomatoes

½ cup finely chopped kalamata olives

½ cup red wine

1 bushel of mushrooms

1 cup walnuts

1 onion

1 Tbsp garlic

1 jar of marinara sauce

1 handful of basil

1 handful of parsley

Salt and pepper to taste

1 Tbsp vegan Worcestershire sauce

1 tsp liquid smoke

½ cup vegan parmesan cheese

In a food processer, pulse mushrooms until finely chopped. In an iron skillet, sauté onions until golden brown. Add garlic and mushrooms and cook for ten minutes. Add vegan Worcestershire sauce and liquid smoke and cook for another few minute's then add wine to deglaze pan. Add walnuts to food processor and pulse until finely chopped. Then add to the pan, along with olives, sun-dried tomatoes and marinara sauce. To finish, add your chopped herbs. Meanwhile grill eggplant, zucchini, and yellow squash. In a lasagna pan, layer with marinara sauce on bottom and line with eggplant, add half of quinoa mixture, top with vegan parmesan cheese. Do the same with zucchini, yellow squash and artichokes with olives. Top with more cheese and bake at 350 degrees for 40 minutes. Enjoy!!

CARROT SOUP WITH BASIL PESTO AND CASHEW PARMESAN CHEESE

This beautiful summer soup pairs nicely with the Irish soda bread!!!

8 large carrots, chopped

1 white potato, chopped

1 onion, diced

2 sprigs of Rosemary, finely chopped

4 sprigs of thyme, finely chopped

1 Tbsp garlic

8 cups veggie broth

1 Tbsp paprika

1 tsp ground ginger

1 tsp turmeric

1 cup Pinot grigio wine

1 Tbsp sunflower oil

Cashew Parmesan cheese:

1 cup cashews

2 Tbsp nutritional yeast

1 tsp parsley

1 tsp garlic powder

1 tsp salt

Add sunflower oil and diced onion to searing hot pan. Add garlic and cook for five minutes. Add in your spices and herbs and continue to cook for a few more minutes. Add in chopped up carrots and potatoes, and cook for 5 to 10 minutes. Deglaze the pan with Pinot grigio wine. Cook for another few minutes, then add veggie broth. Keep on medium-high heat for 20 to 30 minutes until carrots and potatoes are cooked all the way through. Then use an emulsifier or blender and blend soup until smooth. Serve with fresh basil pesto and cashew parmesan cheese (see below).

Put in a blender and blend until it looks like a fine dust. Enjoy!!!

ZIPPORAH'S VEGAN MINESTRONE SOUP

This is a perfect winter soup for a cold winter day! When my sister was pregnant all she wanted was this soup, so we used to cuddle up on the couch and watch "Riverdale" with a big bowl and some homemade bread during the cold Nebraska winter. So this is a shout out to my beautiful little niece.

1 onion, diced

6 cloves of garlic

2 small zucchini

1 yellow squash

2 cans of tomatoes

2 cups cooked barely

2 handfuls of kale, chopped

2 stalks of celery

2 carrots

1 Tbsp tomato paste

1 Tbsp balsamic vinegar

2 Tbsp red wine vinegar

1 cup red wine

6 to 8 cups veggie broth

2 cups beans soaked overnight or boiled on the stove for 45 minutes.

Fresh herb bundle (thyme, oregano, and rosemary) tied together with kitchen string.

Start by sautéing the onions until caramelized, then add balsamic vinegar and cook a few minutes. Add garlic, celery, and carrots. Continue to cook for 5 minutes. Add tomato paste and red wine vinegar. Cook down for a few minutes. Add veggie broth, canned tomatoes, beans and herb bundle and bring to a boil. Once it begins to boil, add barley, zucchini, yellow squash and kale. Let cook on medium high heat for 30 minutes and finish with fresh basil and parsley. Enjoy!!!

PASTA PUTTANESCA

This is inspired by my daughter's favorite book series "A Series of Unfortunate Events."

- 4 heirloom tomatoes, finely chopped
- 1 onion, chopped
- 4 cloves of garlic
- ½ cup kalamata olives
- 4 Tbsp capers
- ¼ cup fresh parsley
- ¼ cup fresh basil
- 1 tsp chili flakes

Start with olive oil and add onion and sauté until brown. Add garlic, chili flakes and tomatoes and cook down for 20 to 30 minutes. Then Add olives, capers and parsley and basil. Cook another 10 minutes. Scoop on top of your favorite pasta and enjoy!!

VEGAN SWEET POTATO AND BLACK BEAN ENCHILADAS

We went on vacation to Red River New Mexico one year and I brought the ingredients to make this and it was a huge hit among my family members.

2 large sweet potatoes, baked and cooled

1 can of black beans, rinsed and drained

1 red pepper diced

1 tsp garlic powder

1 tsp onion powder

1 tsp chili powder

1 tsp cumin

1 lb. of baby Bella mushrooms

1 Tbsp fresh minced garlic

½ cup diced onion

1 Tbsp vegan Worchester

1 tsp liquid smoke

2 Tbsp soy sauce

Salt and pepper

24 corn tortillas (use two per enchilada)

2 bags of vegan cheese

1 recipe for enchilada sauce (see below)

Vegan enchilada sauce:

- 1 red onion, chopped
- 1 Tbsp garlic
- 12 tomatillos
- 2 poblanos
- 1 can of green chiles
- ½ cup veggie broth
- 1 can of diced tomatoes
- 1 Tbsp chili powder
- 1 Tbsp paprika
- 1 Tbsp cumin
- 1 Tbsp oregano

Place tomatillos and the red onion on a lined baking sheet all cut in half. Drizzle with olive oil, salt and pepper. Place in a 400° oven for 20 minutes. Next, take the poblanos and put them on the bottom rack of your oven roasting them whole for 10 to 15 minutes or until blistered. Once the poblanos are well blistered, put them in a small bowl covered with tin foil allowing them to steam for about 5 minutes. After steaming, peel the skin of the poblanos and blend together with tomatillos and onions. Add all other ingredients in a blender and blend until smooth and set aside. Dice the sweet potatoes and line on a cookie sheet with olive oil, chili powder, paprika, cumin, salt and pepper, then bake in the oven for 30 minutes at 400 °. In a skillet on medium high heat add diced onion and cook down until brown then add garlic and the red pepper cooking another few minutes. Add all spices and cook another few minutes then add mushrooms, vegan Worchester, soy sauce, liquid smoke and continue cooking down for another 5 to 10 minutes. Once everything is cooked down, add your black beans and sweet potatoes making sure they are well combined.

To Assemble:

Take 1 cup poblano sauce to the bottom of a casserole pan and spread evenly.

Take your tortilla's two at a time and place a few Tbsp sweet potato filling and sprinkle with your favorite vegan shredded cheese. I like using "Go veggie" because it melts nice and is usually cheaper than other brands. Fold and place folded side down in sauce and continue in a line until all tortillas are gone or pan is filled. Then add the remaining sauce on top with remainder of vegan cheese. Bake in a 400° oven for 20 to 30 minutes until cheese is melted. Top with your favorite vegan sour cream, guacamole and cilantro. Enjoy!!

SOUTHERN "CHICKEN" AND WAFFLES

Homemade southern fried chicken and waffles vegan Style!! I was inspired by the recipe from "bosch" I tweaked it a little to make it my own!!

Waffles:

- 1 can of chickpeas juice (should be about 3/4 of a cup)
- 1/8 tsp cream of tartar
- 2 cups flour
- 1 tsp cinnamon
- 1 tsp salt
- 3 Tbsp brown sugar
- 1 Tbsp baking powder
- 1 ¼ cup plant-based milk
- 1 Tbsp apple cider vinegar
- 1 tsp vanilla

In a small saucepan add chickpea juice and reduce down for 20 minutes until it reaches about half of a cup. this is very important step because the chickpea juice has a lot of starch in it and we're trying to get rid of it before we add it to the mixer. Once cooled completely, add to your KitchenAid mixer and cream of tartar and whisk until stiff White peeks. In a small bowl, add plant-based milk, apple cider vinegar and vanilla; set aside. Mix together your dry ingredients in a large bowl flour, salt, sugar, baking powder until well combined. Add the wet ingredients to dry mixture and whisk again. Add half of the aquafaba egg whites and fold in gently. Mix together the other half of the and fold in gently again. Spray the waffle press and one cup at a time add the batter. Cook until golden brown on each side.

The "Chicken"

- 4 pkgs of oyster mushrooms
- ½ cup plain vegan yogurt
- 1 Tbsp apple cider vinegar
- 1 cup plant-based milk
- 1 cup flour
- 1 tsp paprika
- 1 tsp garlic
- 1 tsp onion powder
- ¼ tsp of nutmeg
- ½ tsp baking soda
- 2 cups coconut oil for frying

Cut mushrooms into quartered pieces then set aside. In a medium sized bowl add your milk, yogurt and apple cider vinegar, then mix until well combined. In a small bowl add your dry ingredients mixing them together. Completely incorporate mushroom pieces in "buttermilk" mixture, cover and set in the fridge for 2 hours. Add your coconut oil to a large cast iron pan and heat on medium high until 350 °. Take your saturated mushrooms out of the fridge and completely coat each one with flour mixture. Then take them, three pieces at a time, and place in the oil until a nice golden brown. Do not overcrowd the "chicken" or they won't cook through properly. Top your "chicken" onto your mound of waffles then douse in agave nectar, maple syrup or whatever your favorite sweetener is.

ROSEMARY FOCACCIA BREAD

Rosemary focaccia bread!! If you've ever wanted to try bread before and you've haven't had any luck, then try this recipe!! It is literally the easiest bread recipe in the world!!

2 cups warm water

1 Tbsp honey

1 Tbsp instant bread machine yeast

3 tsp salt

1 sprig of rosemary, chopped up finely

4 ½ cups flour

½ cup olive oil

In a small bowl, add honey and yeast to one cup warm water set it aside for 10 to 15 minutes to let the yeast start to bubble. Place this in your mixer and add the rest of your ingredients. Mix on low for 10 minutes. Use more olive oil to rub around the bowl and place on top of your oven. Leave the dough there for an hour until doubled in size. then take your dough and place on a cookie sheet with more olive oil on both sides and spread with your fingers until the dough meets the edges of the pan. Generously sprinkle salt and more olive oil on top. Baked in the oven for 20 minutes at 350°. Goes great with minestrone soup!

MY GARDEN'S TOSCANA SOUP

My favorite all-time soup at Olive Garden made vegan!!!

1 bunch of Tuscan kale

2 carrots, shredded

3 leaks, washed liberally, cut in half and chopped

4 russet potatoes, chopped

3 cloves of garlic, finely chopped

1 pkg of plant-based sausage

2 Tbsp flour

8 cups veggie broth

1 can of full-fat coconut milk

1 cup plant-based milk

2 tsp red pepper flakes

2 sprigs of rosemary, finely chopped

2 sprigs of oregano, finely chopped

2 sprigs of thyme, finely chopped

1 bay leaf

2 Tbsp white wine vinegar

1 Tbsp olive oil

Salt and pepper to taste

In a large cast-iron pot start on medium-high heat with olive oil and brown plant-based sausage until cooked all the way through. Remove from pot, add leeks and cook down for a few minutes. Add herbs and garlic and continue to cook down for another few minutes then add white wine vinegar. Add potatoes, then add flour and cook for another few minutes. Add kale, plant-based milk, and cook for another few minutes. Add red pepper flakes salt and pepper and plant-based sausage to the pot then add all of your veggie broth. Cover the pot and Cook for a 20 to 30 minutes. Goes great with focaccia bread!! Enjoy!!

KID APPROVED RATATOUILLE

My kids where watching the Ratatouille movie the other day and asked for this dish. So of course, I had to!! It's actually considered a peasant dish, which is interesting since peasants where the poorest people in the kingdom. So, naturally I love it when people ask me if being vegan is expensive. I simply tell them only if you make it that way.

Sauce:

- 1 can of tomato sauce
- 1 yellow onion, diced
- 4 cloves of garlic, diced
- 1 large handful of fresh basil
- 1 tsp oregano
- 1 tsp basil
- 1 tsp parsley
- 2 Tbsp red wine vinegar
- 1 Tbsp olive oil
- Salt and pepper to taste

In a medium sized cast iron skillet start sweating onions in olive oil for 5 minutes then add garlic. Add salt and pepper and other herbs, and cook another few minutes then add tomato sauce and let it cook for another 5 to 10 minutes. Once finished top with fresh basil.

Ratatouille:

- 1 yellow squash, sliced

- 1 zucchini, sliced

- 1 small eggplant, cut in half then in half again and sliced

- 1 red bell pepper, sliced

- Salt and pepper to taste

- Olive oil

When sauce is done scoop out half of it into a medium sized bowl. Then one at a time, place sliced veggies overlapping each other in a circular motion. When finished, top with olive oil, salt, pepper and your remaining sauce and fresh basil. Place parchment paper over pan and bake in 400°oven for 20 minutes. Eat as is or add it to your favorite pasta!! Enjoy!!

VEGAN FAJITAS

Marinated portobello mushrooms, sliced zucchini, red onion and red and orange bell peppers makes for an awesome weekend meal!!

Marinade:

- The juice of one orange
- Juice of one lime
- 2 Tbsp soy sauce
- 1 Tbsp vegan Worcestershire sauce
- 1 tsp liquid smoke
- 1 Tbsp fajita seasoning
- 1 tsp paprika
- 1 tsp Mexican oregan

Take the stem out of the mushroom and devein it. Then slice the mushrooms as thick as you like and set aside. Place all of your other ingredients in a medium sized bowl and whisk until well combined. Then add your mushrooms and toss until they are completely coated and place back in the refrigerator for about 1 hour. Slice zucchini, bell pepper, onion garlic and set aside. In a medium-sized pan at your red onion and olive oil salt and pepper to taste and begin to char The Onion until completely caramelized for about 10 to 15 minutes. Then add your mushrooms with the marinade to the pan and cook down for another 5 minutes. Then add the rest of your veggies and cook another 5 minutes. I used whole wheat tortillas, salsa, guacamole, cilantro, and Vegan sour cream. Enjoy!!

ROASTED VEGGIE PASTA BAKE

This was literally a last-minute throw everything together in one pot meal. It ended up being a hit in my house.

Roasted veggies:

- 1 large red bell pepper
- 1 large zucchini
- 1 large eggplant

Chop all veggies roughly, and place on a cookie sheet. Drizzle with olive oil salt and pepper to taste. Roast in the oven at 400° for 40 minutes.

Sauce:

- 1 large jar of your favorite marinara sauce
- 2 cans of tomato sauce
- 2 Tbsp tomato paste
- 1 onion
- 3 Tbsp garlic
- 2 Tbsp red wine vinegar
- 1 bunch of fresh basil chopped
- 1 Tbsp dried oregano
- 1 Tbsp dried parsley
- Salt and pepper to taste

In a large saucepan on high heat, place chopped onion in the pan with salt and pepper. Cook down until onions become caramelized, roughly about 10 to 12 minutes. Add and garlic, oregano, parsley and red wine vinegar, tomato paste and cook down for another 5 minutes. Add marinara sauce and tomato sauce and fresh basil and place heat on low for another 10 minutes. Add your favorite cooked pasta, and roasted veggies mixed, together until combined and place in a casserole dish with go veggie mozzarella cheese and vegan Parmesan cheese on top. Place in the oven at 400° for 20 minutes and garnish with parsley. Enjoy!!!

CHICKEN-LESS CHICKEN SOUP

Nothing says comfort food like some good ole fashioned chicken noodle soup!! So, grab your comfy blanket and snuggle up on the couch with some homemade bread and a bowl of this and you'll feel right at home!!!

1 can of chickpeas, rinsed and drained

2 carrots, chopped

4 stalks of celery, chopped

1 onion, chopped

1 Tbsp garlic

4 cups kale, finely chopped

1 handful of parsley, chopped

1 Tbsp rosemary

1 tsp thyme

6 cups veggie broth

2 cups water

1 Tbsp white wine vinegar

2 cups chickpea pasta

Salt and pepper to taste

Turn Instapot on sauté, and add onion and cook a few minutes. Add all other ingredients except for the kale. Close the lid and make sure the pressure button is secure. Press the soup button and leave it for 30 minutes. Release the pressure valve when done and throw in the kale. Let the kale steep for 5 minutes then serve. Enjoy!!!

MY BFF'S BUTTERNUT SQUASH SOUP

So good and so fitting for fall!!! Its sweater weather time!!

- 1 onion, chopped
- 1 Tbsp garlic
- 1 whole butternut squash
- 1 Tbsp fresh rosemary
- 1 Tbsp fresh thyme
- 2 carrots, finely chopped
- 2 stalks of celery, finely chopped
- 1 tsp allspice
- ½ cup white wine
- 1 Tbsp white wine vinegar
- 4 cups veggie broth
- 1 can of coconut milk
- Salt and pepper to taste

Cut the butternut squash in half and de-seed it. Place on a cookie sheet with salt, pepper and olive oil and roast in the oven for 30 to 45 minutes Temp? and set aside, let cool completely. Add 1 Tbsp olive oil or veggie broth to the pan and add onion. Salt onion immediately so it continues to sweat down. Add garlic and rosemary and thyme let cook down for a few minutes.

Add celery and carrots and cook another few minutes. While that's cooking, peel the skin off butternut squash and place in a blender with coconut milk and blend until smooth. Add white wine and vinegar to the onions, carrots and celery and let cook a few more minutes. Add the butternut squash to the pan of onions, carrots and celery with four cups veggie broth. Use a whisk to combine and let cook for 30 minutes. Leave soup as is and eat on its own or add to the blender again and blend until smooth.

PESTO STUFFED TOMATOES

I once saw Racheal Ray fix stuffed tomatoes on the food network channel and fell in love with the idea. So, this is my version and it just so happens to be a great crowd pleaser.

Pesto:

  ½ cup olive oil

  2 handfuls of fresh basil

  ¼ cup cashews

  2 Tbsp nutritional yeast

  The juice of one lemon

  Salt and pepper

Combine all ingredients in a blender and blend until smooth. Set aside.

Stuffing for tomatoes:

Cut the tops off of eight tomatoes. Scoop out the insides and put in a bowl, set aside. Place the scooped-out tomatoes in a baking pan.

  1 cup quinoa

  2 cups veggie broth

Cook quinoa and veggie broth for 20 minutes on medium high heat. Set aside.

  1 red onion, chopped

  The insides of the tomatoes chopped

1 whole bag of spinach

1 can of artichoke hearts

2 Tbsp garlic

1 Tbsp red wine vinegar

1 tsp basil

1 tsp oregano

1 tsp thyme

1 tsp parsley

¼ cup breadcrumbs

1 Tbsp nutritional yeast

In a pan on medium-high heat add 1 Tbsp olive oil and red onion and sauté until gold and brown. Add garlic and sauté for 2 more minutes. Add the chopped tomatoes, artichoke hearts and spinach and sauté for another 5 minutes. Add red wine vinegar and dried herbs and sauté for another 5 minutes. Then add your quinoa and pesto. Turn off heat and add to the inside of your tomatoes. Combine bread crumbs and nutritional yeast an add to the top of your tomatoes with drizzled olive oil. Baked in the oven for 20 to 30 minutes. Enjoy!!

CARROT HOT DOGS

Hey moms!! My kids didn't even know the difference!!

One bag of carrots

½ cup soy sauce

¼ cup balsamic vinegar

1 tsp liquid smoke

¼ cup maple syrup

2 tsp vegan Worcestershire sauce

1 tsp onion powder

1 tsp garlic powder

1 tsp smoked paprika

Peel and cut off the ends of each carrot. Bring a large pot of water to boil and salt liberally before adding the carrots. Parboil the whole carrots for 10 minutes then take them out to dry. In a medium size baking dish add all of your ingredients and mix thoroughly until well combined. Then add your carrots to the marinade and let it sit for 2 hours in the fridge flipping every 30 minutes so that all sides are coated. On a grill on medium-high heat, add carrots and grill for 2 to 4 minutes on each side. Goes great with my kid approved mac and cheese. Add your favorite toppings and enjoy!!

CREAMY POTATO SOUP

Creamy potato soup with kale chips!! This is a beautifully light and creamy soup ready for the spring.

- 4 potatoes, peeled and cubed
- 2 carrots, chopped
- 3 stalks of celery, chopped
- 1 onion, diced
- 2 cloves of garlic, minced
- 1 Tbsp herb de Provence
- The juice of half a lemon
- ½ cup white wine
- 16 oz of veggie broth
- 16 oz of water
- 2 Tbsp olive oil
- Salt and pepper to taste

In a large stock pot on medium-high heat, add olive oil, onion and garlic. Cook for 5 to 10 minutes until translucent. Add carrots and celery and cook another 2 minutes. Add herbs de Provence, salt and pepper. Deglaze the pan with white wine. I added your potatoes then Add veggie broth and water and cook on low heat for 30 minutes. Once the potatoes are fully cooked, add everything to a blender and blend until smooth, Then add the lemon. Garnish with kale chips and enjoy!!

Kale chips:

- 2 bushels of kale chopped
- 2 Tbsp olive oil
- 1 tsp garlic powder
- 1 tsp onion powder
- Salt and pepper to taste

Chop the kale evenly then add to a cookie sheet. Drizzle with olive oil and evenly spread the garlic and onion powder. Add salt and pepper to taste. Place in a 400° oven for 20 minutes.

GRANDDADS TEXAS CHILI AND CORNBREAD

My father-in-law loves a good chili and cornbread dinner. I agree on a chilly day, nothing's better than a bowl of three bean chili and some jalapeno corn bread!!

1 can black beans

1 can pinto beans

1 can kidney beans

2 cans diced tomatoes

6 cups veggie broth

1 can tomato paste

1 Tbsp vegan Worcestershire sauce

1 onion, chopped

2 carrots, chopped

2 stalks of celery, chopped

1 Tbsp garlic

1 red pepper chopped

1 Tbsp chili powder

1 tsp cumin

1 tsp paprika

1 tsp onion powder

1 tsp garlic powder

½ tsp cayenne pepper

1 avocado

Dairy-free sour cream

In a cast iron 8-quart pan on medium high heat and add the onions, salt and pepper. Wait until onion starts to caramelize then add carrots and celery. Let cook down for a few minutes then add garlic and spices. Add tomato paste and cook for another five minutes and add vegan Worcestershire sauce and cook another few minutes. Rinse and drain all beans and add them along with the canned tomatoes, and veggie broth. Let cook down for 30 minutes and then enjoy!!!

HOMEMADE JALAPENO CHEDDAR BREAD!!

1 onion, chopped

1 jalapeno, de-seeded and chopped

½ cup vegan cheddar cheese

1 cup of flour

1 cup corn bread

1 flaxseed egg (1 Tbsp flaxseed and 2 Tbsp water set aside for 5 minutes)

2 tsp baking soda

2 tsp baking powder

1 tsp salt

1 cup plant-based milk

Sauté chopped onion and jalapeno in a cast iron skillet until caramelized. While that's cooking, whisk all dry ingredients in a bowl then add flaxseed egg and milk and cheese. Pour batter over the onions and jalapenos in skillet. Place in a 350°oven for 30 to 40 minutes until golden brown on top. Enjoy!!!

BETTER THAN MOMS VEGAN MEATLOAF

My biggest hit on my Facebook page was this recipe right here. Enough said.

1 cup lentils

2 cups veggie broth

I cook mine in my Instapot on the brown rice setting, or cook on stove for 20 to 30 minutes.

1 onion

2 Tbsp garlic

2 carrots

2 stalks of celery

2 cups mushrooms

¼ cup veggie broth

1 Tbsp tomato paste

1 tsp vegan Worcestershire sauce

1/8 tsp liquid smoke

1 tsp paprika

1 tsp thyme

1 cup flour

½ cup vegan barbecue sauce

salt and pepper to taste

In a food processor, add onions, celery and carrots and pulse them until very fine. Next, add olive oil, onions, garlic, carrots, and celery in a sauté pan on medium high heat. Cook down for 5-10 minutes. While cooking, add the mushrooms to the food processor and pulse until fine. Then add the veggie broth and mushrooms and continue cooking another 5-10 minutes or until tender. Add to the pan, paprika, thyme, salt and pepper, vegan Worcestershire sauce, tomato paste and liquid smoke, then cook down for another 5 minutes. While waiting for that to finish, blend in a food processor the cooked lentils and place them in a medium sized bowl with the flour, salt and pepper. Add your cooked ingredients with the lentils and flour, then mix until completely combined. Place in a loaf pan and top with barbecue sauce. In a 350° oven cook for 45 minutes to 1 hour. Enjoy!!!

WALDER FREY "MEAT" PIE

Game of Thrones Veggie Walder Frey pie, because I'm a nerd. No worries, it's completely meat free. No fingers or toes in this recipe!!

1 onion, chopped

1 Tbsp olive oil

4 cloves of garlic

2 tsp sage

2 tsp rosemary

2 tsp thyme

1 Tbsp paprika

12 fingerling potatoes (Because you know)

2 lbs. of baby portobello mushrooms

1 cup walnuts

2 carrots

4 stalks of celery

1 Tbsp tomato paste

3 Tbsp flour

1 cup marsala wine

3 Tbsp vegan Worcestershire

2 cups veggie broth

2 sheets of vegan puffed pastry or pie dough

Put mushrooms and walnuts in food processor and pulse until well combined. In a large pan add olive oil and add diced onions, cook down until caramelized. Add garlic and cook a few more minutes. Then add mushroom and walnut mixture. Cook down on medium high heat for 20 minutes until moisture from the mushrooms is gone. Add sage, Rosemary, thyme and paprika, then add tomato paste and vegan Worcestershire sauce and cook down for 5 more minutes. Add marsala wine and cook down another 2 minutes. Add carrots and celery and potatoes. Sprinkle flour in and cook another few minutes. Add veggie broth and cook for another few minutes.

Take puffed pastry and roll out and form around cheesecake pan. Roll out the second puffed pastry set aside. Add mushroom mixture to cheesecake pan and take second pastry and cover. Cut the extra pastry off and tuck in around the edges. Cut an x in the middle and put in a 350° oven for 45 minutes to 1 hour.

BLACK BEAN TACOS

Because Taco Tuesday happens every week in this family!!

- 1 onion, chopped
- 1 Tbsp garlic
- 1 green pepper (or jalapeno)
- 1 Tbsp chili powder
- 1 Tbsp paprika
- 1 Tbsp cumin
- 1/8 tsp cayenne pepper
- 2 Tbsp veggie broth
- 4 cups cooked beans

Start with a pan on medium-high heat and add your onion and sweat it out for 2 to 4 minutes.

Add green pepper and garlic. Cook a few more minutes and then add veggie broth to deglaze the pan. Then add beans and continue cooking. Mash beans with a potato masher and add more veggie broth if needed. Fuse in corn tortillas and add your favorite taco toppings!! Enjoy!!!

sides are coated. Then on a grill on medium-high heat add carrots and grill for 2 to 4 minutes on each side. Add your favorite toppings and enjoy!!

557TH WEATHER WING NEW ORLEANS STYLE GUMBO

We were stationed down at Keesler AFB, Mississippi for a few years and as much as I hated the heat and bugs, I got the privilege of watching a little old man make his families recipe of gumbo one night. This is my version of his gumbo, veganized, and of course it goes great with my jalapeno cornbread!! One year in particular while my husband was deployed, we found out we had to move houses because of plumbing issues. I asked my husband's squadron if they helped us move, I would make them Gumbo and cornbread in return. We had a dozen Airmen

show up and help us move that day and I will always be grateful for their help. So, here's to the men and women of the 557th Weather Wing at Offutt AFB Nebraska.

2 packages of Beyond beef sausages sliced

1 jar of hearts of palm peeled and shredded (Marinade in a small bowl with 2 tsp of nori furikake)

2 cans of Jackfruit rinsed and drained

2 lbs of sliced mushrooms

1 28oz can of crushed tomatoes

1 can of tomato paste

1 large onion diced

4 stalks of celery diced

1 large green bell pepper diced

2 tablespoons of garlic

A few tablespoons of Louisiana hot sauce (Give or take however spicey you like it)

2 tablespoons of Cajun Street seasoning

1 tablespoon of apple cider vinegar

1 stick of vegan butter

2 tablespoons of sunflower oil

1\2 cup of all-purpose flour

2 tablespoons of vegan Worcestershire sauce

2 teaspoons of liquid smoke

1 Tablespoon of smoked paprika

1 teaspoon of cayenne pepper

1 tablespoon of oregano

2 bags of frozen okra

2 cups of frozen corn

6 cups of veggie broth

Start off with a little oil in the bottom of your biggest stock pot, and add your sausages and begin to brown on both sides. Add a tablespoon of Louisiana hot sauce and a tablespoon of Cajun seasoning and cook down for a few minutes. With a slotted spoon scoop out sausages and set aside. Then do the same thing with the jackfruit. Once the jackfruit is done place it on a cookie sheet and spread out evenly, then place in a 400 degree oven for 20 minutes.

Then take your vegan butter and add it to the pan and scrap up all the little tidbits from the bottom of the pan. Once its melted add your flour and begin to cook down for 10 to 20 minutes give or take however long it takes to achieve a caramel like color. This is called a rue, and yes it does take a little patience but its so worth it. Once your rue is ready add your onion, celery and green bell pepper. This is called the holy trinity in New Orleans. And cook down for 5 minutes till veggies begin to soften. Add your garlic and tomato paste and cook down another few minutes. Then add your cider vinegar, Worcestershire sauce, and liquid smoke and cook down again for another few minutes. Add another tablespoon of Cajun seasoning, and all your other spices as well as another tablespoon of Louisiana hot sauce. Now add your canned tomatoes, veggie broth, mushrooms, corn, and okra. Take your jackfruit out of the oven and add it to the pot with your sausages and hearts or palm. Cook down for 30 minutes to an hour. Now the longer it sits the better it gets, so usually I make this the day before and let it sit overnight in the fridge then reheat it the next day. That's when it tastes the best but you do you honey and enjoy!!

VEGAN CHOCOLATE MOUSSE

I made this for my mother-in-law and she fell head over heels for it!! It's a winner after dinner party dessert.

- **4 ripe avocados**
- **½ cup cocoa powder**
- **4 Tbsp maple syrup**
- **1 tsp vanilla extract**

Blend all ingredients in a blender or food processor. Serve in small bowls and chill for 1 hour in fridge. Top with your favorite berries!!!

GRILLED PEACH ICE CREAM WITH TURMERIC

Here's an awesome anti-inflammatory ice cream for national ice cream day!!!

Turmeric latte:

- 1 can of full fat coconut milk
- 3 Tbsp maple syrup
- 1 tsp turmeric
- 1 tsp of black peppercorns
- 4 Peaches grilled on both sides.
- ½ tsp ground ginger
- 6 black peppercorns

Heat on stove on medium high heat until steamed. Then strain and serve in a mug. Great before bedtime!! Helps with inflammation and sleeplessness.

Or Add all of the ingredients except peaches to a saucepan on medium high heat and simmer for 15 minutes then set aside and let it cool all the way. Take a loaf pan and grease all sides and add your ingredients from the sauce pan. Freeze in the freezer for 2 hours then scoop in a bowl and add your peaches and chopped walnuts if desired. Enjoy!!

HARRY POTTER'S NO MELT ICE CREAM

Anyone who knows me knows I am a nerd and I love Harry Potter!! So, we always have Harry Potter nights filled with all the special treats from Hogsmeade!!

1 stick of vegan butter

½ cup brown sugar

1 tsp vanilla

1 tsp rum extract

1 Tbsp agave nectar

2 Tbsp plant-based milk

1 cup almond flour

½ cup vegan chocolate chips

In a food processor beat together butter and sugar until well combined then add vanilla, agave nectar, milk, and flour. Then place dough in a separate bowl and gently stir in vegan chocolate chips. Scoop into bowls and top with melted vegan chocolate!!

MRS. WEASLEY'S PUMPKIN PASTIES

For the dough:

- 1 cup flour

- 1/3 cup Crisco

- 1 tsp salt

- 1 tsp cinnamon

- 2 tablespoons brown sugar

- 3-6 Tbsp ice cold water (varies based on altitude)

In a medium sized bowl with a fork, mash the flour and Crisco until it resembles a dry oatmeal. Add the brown sugar, salt and cinnamon, then, slowly add the cold water, 1 tablespoon at a time, and stir until you have a firm pie dough. Roll out the dough to ¼ of an inch and cut into 8 large triangles.

For the pumpkin filling:

- 3/4 can of pumpkin

- ½ cup brown sugar

- ¼ cup cornstarch

- 2 tsp pumpkin pie spice

- 1 tsp vanilla extract

In a medium sized bowl, add all the ingredients and whisk until completely combined. Add 2 Tbsp worth of the filling to the middle of each triangle shaped dough, then cover with another identical piece. Crimp the outlines of the doughs together then cut a crisscross pattern on the top before baking. Place in the oven at 375 ° for 10-15 minutes or until golden brown.

FRUIT PIZZA WITH CHIA SEED PUDDING

My kids love this fruit pizza, it's not only fun to make but fun to eat as well.

Dough:

- Pizza dough, (I made my own but you can use store bought)
- 2 Tbsp vegan butter
- 2 Tbsp cinnamon and sugar

Roll out dough in the shape of a pizza, then spread with butter, cinnamon and sugar and bake in a 400° oven for 20 minutes and let cool.

Chia seed pudding:

- ¼ cup chia seeds
- 1 can of coconut cream
- 1 vanilla bean, split in half and seeds taken out
- ¼ cup agave nectar

In a saucepan add coconut cream, vanilla bean and agave nectar and heat until well combined. Remove from heat and place in a small bowl. Add chia seeds and cover with plastic wrap and refrigerate overnight.

To assemble:

Add chia seed pudding to the already baked pizza crust and line up strawberries and blueberries however you like. Drizzle with agave nectar and enjoy!!

CHOCOLATE BANANA ICE CREAM

This is a great idea for breakfast in the mourning for the kids. Who doesn't love ice-cream for breakfast!!

- 4 frozen bananas
- 2 Tbsp raw cacao powder
- ¼ cup agave nectar
- 1 tsp vanilla extract
- 4 Tbsp full fat coconut milk

I put the can of coconut milk in the fridge overnight so the milk and water separate. Scrape the top layer of the plant-based milk and use that and use the water for another recipe. Blend all ingredients in blender until smooth. Place in the freezer for 2 hours. Top with walnuts and grilled pineapple!!

VEGAN LEMON BARS

These were my favorite childhood sweet treats growing up!!

For the shortbread cookie dough

- 1 cup flour
- ½ cup melted vegan butter
- ¼ cup sugar in the raw
- ½ tsp salt
- 1 tsp almond extract

Combine all ingredients in a medium sized bowl until dough is formed. In an 8"X 8" pan spray with cooking spray. Press your cookie dough into the pan until every inch is covered on the bottom. Then place in a 350° oven for 10 minutes.

Lemon custard filling:

- 1 cup sugar in the raw
- 1 can of full-fat coconut milk
- ½ cup freshly squeezed lemon juice
- The zest of two lemons
- 6 Tbsp Bob mills egg replacer
- 3 Tbsp cornstarch

In a sauce pan on medium-high heat add sugar, coconut milk, egg replacer and cornstarch and whisk until well combined. Cook for 2 minutes until custard starts to come together then add the lemon juice and lemon zest. you want to wait until this part to add your lemon juice because the egg replacer has baking soda in it and it will fizz up all over your stove. Cook for another 2 to 3 minutes then take it off the heat and set aside for a few minutes. Add to your 8"X 8" pan with the shortbread cookie dough. Then placed back in the oven for another 5 minutes then let it cool completely in the fridge for 4 to 6 hours. Dust with powdered sugar and enjoy!!

KASHA'S BANANA BREAD

I've been making banana bread for over 10 years now, and it is by far one of my favorite things to make. I always make it with a buttermilk so just add some apple cider vinegar to your favorite plant-based milk and microwave it for a minute does the trick perfectly.

2 cups flour

3 over ripe bananas, mashed

1 cup plant-based milk

1 Tbsp apple cider vinegar

1 stick of melted plant-based butter

1 tsp baking powder

1 tsp baking soda

1 tsp cinnamon

½ tsp salt

½ brown sugar

In a small bowl add milk and apple cider vinegar and place in the microwave for 1 minute and set aside. Mash bananas in the bottom of a medium sized bowl, then add milk mixture, sugar, and butter and mix until well combined. In a separate bowl, add the dry ingredients and mix well. Slowly whisk together with wet ingredients. In the bottom of the loaf pans, spray with olive oil cooking spray and then sprinkle with cinnamon and sugar. this step is important because it caramelizes on the bottom and gives it a nice crust. Then add the batter and place sliced bananas on top, and sprinkle with more cinnamon and sugar. Bake in a 350° oven for 40 to 50 minutes. Enjoy!!

VEGAN MARDI GRAS KINGS CAKE

Happy Mardi gras!!! Vegan Kings cake is basically a giant cinnamon roll with confetti. It's so much fun to make with the kids.

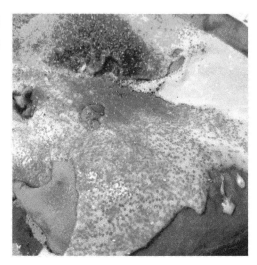

Filling:

- 2 sticks of plant-based butter
- 1 cup brown sugar
- 1 Tbsp cinnamon

Mix all ingredients in a bowl until smooth and combined.

Icing:

- 2 cups powdered sugar
- 2 Tbsp plant-based milk
- 1 tsp vanilla extract

Mix all ingredients in a small bowl until well combined.

Dough:

- 2 Tbsp active rise Yeast
- 2 cups warm water
- 4 ½ cups flour
- 1 stick of softened plant-based butter
- 1 tsp cinnamon
- 2 Tbsp agave nectar

In a bowl add yeast, agave nectar, and water and leave it on the top of the oven for 10 to 15 minutes to rise. Add the rest of your ingredients, adding flour 1 cup at a time. Knead dough for 10 minutes. Place back in bowl and let it rise for 90 minutes. Once dough has doubled in size, dust the counter with flour and cut the dough in half. Roll out on counter until ¼ of an inch thick, then spread half of the filling mixture. Roll up and shape into a doughnut. Let rise for another thirty minutes, then place in the oven for 35 minutes at 350°. Let cool for drizzle icing on top of cake and add sprinkles!! Enjoy!!

MERRICK'S SWEET POTATO BROWNIES

One of my son's favorite desserts has to be brownies! I used to always burn brownies made from the box for some reason. But since I found by adding the sweet potatoes not only keeps it moist but adds extra sweetness as well. This is by far one of my favorite brownie recipes I've ever found and it's all vegan!!

1 cup sweet potato, mashed

1 cup of flour

1/3 cup plant-based milk

1 tsp baking soda

1 tsp baking powder

½ tsp salt

1 tsp vanilla

2 Tbsp cocoa powder

½ cup a vegan chocolate chips

½ cup coconut oil

1 flax seed egg (1 Tbsp flaxseed ground and two Tbsp water set aside for 10 minutes)

In a medium sized bowl, mix together mashed sweet potato, milk, flaxseed egg, until well combined. Then take all of your dry ingredients and mix them in a separate bowl. Then slowly add your dry ingredients to your wet ingredients and lastly your chocolate chips and stir them until well combined. In a square 8"X 8" pan, spray with olive oil spray and spread the batter evenly. Place the pan in a 350° oven for 30 minutes. Enjoy!!

CHOCOLATE CHICKPEA COOKIES AND STAR WARS MILK

May the force be with you!! Chickpea chocolate chip cookies and Star Wars milk!! Need I say more!!

Cookie dough:

- 1 can of chickpeas, rinsed and drained
- 1/3 cup maple syrup
- 1 tsp almond extract
- ½ cup vegan chocolate chips
- 3/4 cup peanut butter
- 1 tsp baking powder

Blend all of the ingredients in a food processor except for the chocolate chips. Once everything is combined stir in the chocolate chips. On a cookie sheet, lined it with parchment paper and scoop out of cookie dough 1 Tbsp at a time. Flatten with a fork. Place in 350° oven for 10 to 12 minutes.

Star Wars milk:

- 1 cup frozen pineapple
- 1 cup frozen mango
- 1 can of full fat coconut milk
- 1 cup plant-based milk
- 3 drops of blue dye
- 3 cups ice
- 1 cup pineapple juice

Blend all ingredients in a blender except for blue dye and ice. Once the other ingredients are combined add your dye and blend again. Then add your ice chips and blend once more until well combined.

CHRISTMAS VEGAN PUMPKIN ROLL

My father-in-law made me a pumpkin roll one Christmas and I have been making them every year since. Merry Christmas and happy holidays from my home to yours!!!

1 ½ cups flour

1/3 cup chickpea juice from the can

½ banana

1 Tbsp cinnamon

1 tsp nutmeg

1 tsp allspice

1 tsp baking powder

2 tsp baking soda

2/3 cup coconut cream

3/4 cup canned pumpkin

1 tsp vanilla extract

3 Tbsp coconut oil

Mash banana well in a medium sized bowl, then add chickpea juice and whip for 3 minutes. Add coconut oil, vanilla, coconut cream, and pumpkin and whip together until combined. Add cinnamon, nutmeg, allspice, baking powder, baking soda, flour and gently fold until combined.

Take a baking sheet with wax paper and spray with cooking spray. Then add cake mixture and gently smooth out. Place in a 350°oven for 20 to 30 minutes. When toothpick comes out clean take it out of the oven. Let it cool for just a few minutes then place on top of another piece of wax paper and roll into a log and place in the fridge for 1 hour to overnight.

Cream cheese filling:

- 1 can of coconut milk
- 1 Tbsp lemon juice
- ¼ of a tsp salt
- ½ of powdered sugar
- 1 tsp cinnamon
- 1 stick of plant-based butter

I place the can of coconut milk in the fridge overnight so the milk and water separate. Take the coconut milk and skim the top of the cream do not use the water on the bottom of the can. Place in a small bowl and whip until smooth then add lemon juice and salt and set in the fridge for 1 hour. Whip the softened butter in a medium sized bowl and add sugar and cinnamon. When cream cheese is formed, strain using a strainer and cheesecloth. Squeeze as much of the water out as you possibly can. Then add to butter and sugar mix and whip together until combined. Take pumpkin roll out of the fridge and gently unroll and spread cream cheese filling. Gently roll up while removing the wax paper. Place on a platter and refrigerate again for another hour. Enjoy!!

VEGAN AVOCADO CHOCOLATE PIE

My daughter Avanlea is a huge fan of chocolate pie so we decided to make this for her.

Crust:

- 1 pkg of cinnamon honey Graham crackers
- 1 cup walnuts
- 1 cup melted plant-based butter

Blend all in a food processor until smooth and place in a pie dish and press down until even.

Filling:

- 4 ripe avocados
- 1 cup vegan chocolate chips, melted
- 2 Tbsp dark cocoa powder
- 3 Tbsp sugar
- 1 tsp vanilla

Blend all ingredients in a blender except for blue dye and ice. Once the other ingredients are combined add your dye and blend again. Then add your ice chips and blend once more until well combined.

Whipping cream:

- 1 can of coconut cream (I only use the cream fill on top of the can do not add the water at the bottom. To get this effect place the can in the fridge overnight.)
- 2 tsp arrowroot or xanthan gum
- 3 tsp powdered sugar

I place my bowl that I'm whipping it in in the freezer for 30 minutes then place all your ingredients in the bowl and whip for about 5 to 10 minutes. Place on top of your pie and garnish with shaved chocolate and crushed candy canes!! Enjoy!!!

MRS. OHMES HOMEMADE PUMPKIN PIE

So, I have made my own pumpkin puree for my pumpkin pies ever since I was 14. I learned this recipe from a dear friend of mine growing up. I never make pumpkin pie any other way, it's so worth it!! And easier than people think.

Pumpkin puree:

- 1 pumpkin, de-seeded and cut into several pieces
- Cinnamon for dusting
- Vegan butter cut into tablespoons

Place pieces of pumpkin onto foil, add 1 tablespoon vegan butter and dust with cinnamon and wrap in foil. Place in a 350° oven for 1 hour. Then take out and let it cool completely. I will usually do this the night before and let it cool overnight and puree in food processor in the morning. Place in individual jars and refrigerate or can in a canner.

Crust:

- 1/3 cup Crisco
- 1 cup all-purpose flour
- 2 tablespoons of brown sugar
- 4 to 6 Tbsp ice cold water
- ½ tsp salt

Place all dry ingredients in a medium size bowl and whisk together. Add Crisco and with a fork mash together until it resembles dry oatmeal. Add ice water one TBSP at a time, give or take how the weather is depends on how much you actually need to add. Make sure its not too sticky and not too dry. Needs to resemble play-dough. Use hands to bring it together, the dough should lick the bowl clean when ready. Roll out and place in pie pan.

Pumpkin pie:

- 1-8 oz jar of pumpkin puree
- ½ cup brown sugar
- 1 Tbsp pumpkin pie spice
- ½ can of full fat coconut milk
- 1 tsp cinnamon
- 1/8 cup cornstarch (egg replacement)

Whisk all ingredients together in a medium size bowl. Then place in pie crust and bake at 350° for 1 hour. Enjoy!!!

VEGAN SUGAR COOKIES

You can't celebrate the holidays without making some over-the-top amazing sugar cookies!!

Cookie dough:

- 1 stick of plant-based butter
- ½ cup sugar
- ½ cup brown sugar
- ½ cup applesauce (egg substitute)
- 1 tsp baking powder
- 1 tsp baking soda
- ½ tsp salt
- 1 Tbsp cornstarch
- 2 tsp almond milk
- 1 tsp vanilla
- 2 cups all-purpose flour

Frosting:

- 2 sticks of plant-based butter
- 2 cups powdered sugar
- 1 tsp vanilla

In a large mixing bowl cream together plant-based butter and both sugars until well combined. Add the applesauce and mix again. Add baking powder, baking soda, salt, cornstarch, vanilla, and almond milk and mixed together. Then add two cups flour, slowly. The dough should remind you of a pie dough, firm and not sticky. Wrap and plastic wrap and place in the fridge for one hour or overnight for best results. Take the dough out of the fridge and with a little extra flour, roll out into your favorite cookie cutter shapes. Baked in the oven for 7 to 10 minutes at 350 degrees. Enjoy!!

Beat together the two sticks of butter until creamy, then add sugar and vanilla and beat until well combined. I put mine in separate bowls and added my own colored dyes. Then I place them in little Ziplock baggies and cut the corners. This makes it an easy cleanup with kids. Add your favorite sprinkles and enjoy!!!

NANA'S VEGAN GINGER CRINKLE COOKIES

Vegan gingersnap cookies were my absolute favorite holiday cookie growing up. I always asked my Nana to make them every year!!

2 sticks of plant-based butter

2 cup brown sugar

½ cup molasses

1 cup pumpkin puree

1 Tbsp ginger

1 Tbsp cinnamon

1 tsp nutmeg

1 Tbsp baking soda

½ tsp salt

3 cups flour

1 cup sugar, set aside in a bowl

Beat butter and brown sugar together until well combined then add molasses and pumpkin puree and beat again until well combined. Add the ginger, cinnamon, nutmeg, baking soda, salt and stir again until combined then one cup at a time add the flour. Once everything is well combined the dough should be nice and firm well enough to make into little balls. Once you've rolled out all your dough into little balls place them one at a time in sugar filled bowl and toss evenly and place on a baking sheet, press with a fork crisscross and bake for 10 to 12minutes at what temp? Enjoy!!!

ST. PATRICK'S ROASTED CABBAGE

My husband recently found out that both sides of his family are Irish, so naturally I had to make this in celebration of this discovery!!!

1 large head of cabbage

3 Tbsp olive oil

1 Tbsp Dijon mustard

1 stick of vegan butter

2 tsp maple syrup

1 tsp vegan Worcestershire sauce (optional)

1 Tbsp garlic

2 stalks celery, cut into quarters

2 medium carrots, peeled and cut into thirds

½ yellow onion, cut into quarters

1 Tbsp extra-virgin olive oil

1 Tbsp freshly chopped sage

1 Tbsp freshly chopped rosemary

1 Tbsp freshly chopped thyme

½ cup veggie broth, divided

1 Tbsp freshly chopped parsley, for garnish

Gravy:

- 4 Tbsp olive oil
- ½ onion, finely chopped
- 4 oz baby Bella mushrooms, finely chopped
- 1 tsp freshly chopped sage
- 1 tsp freshly chopped rosemary
- 1 tsp freshly chopped thyme
- 3 Tbsp all-purpose flour
- 3 cups veggie broth

Cut stem(core out of) cabbage so it can sit flat. In a medium bowl, whisk together melted butter, mustard, maple syrup, vegan Worcestershire, and garlic powder, and season liberally with salt and pepper. In a large bowl, combine celery, carrots, onion, oil, and chopped herbs. Season with salt and pepper and toss to coat. Place vegetable mixture in a large, oven-safe skillet. Nestle cabbage in the center, on top of the vegetables, and brush all over with half the melted butter mixture. Pour half of vegetable broth into the bottom of the skillet and cover cabbage with aluminum foil. Bake for 45 minutes at 400°. After 45 minutes, remove foil and brush with remaining butter mixture. Add remaining ¼ cup broth and bake 45 minutes more, until cabbage is tender and slightly charred. (Pierce cabbage with a paring knife to check if it's tender.)

Meanwhile, to make gravy: In a small saucepan over medium heat, melt butter, add onion and cook, stirring until soft for 6 minutes. Stir in mushrooms and herbs. Season with salt and pepper. Cook, stirring occasionally, until mushrooms are soft and golden, about 4 minutes. Stir in flour and cook 1 minute, then whisk in 3 cups broth and bring mixture to a boil. Reduce heat to low and simmer until mixture has thickened to your desired consistency, about 5 minutes. Pour over sliced cabbage and your favorite mashed potatoes. Enjoy!!

MY HUBBY'S SHEPHARD'S PIE

May the luck of the Irish be with you!! I hope you get a chance to try out this awesome shepherd's pie recipe!!

1 ½ cup lentils

2 carrots, diced

2 stalks of celery, diced

1 large onion, diced

2 Tbsp garlic, minced

1 cup frozen corn

1 cup frozen peas

2 Tbsp vegan butter

2 Tbsp olive oil

16 oz of veggie broth

1 can of diced tomatoes

1 Tbsp tomato paste

1 Tbsp vegan Worcestershire sauce

1 cup red wine

1 Tbsp fresh thyme

1 Tbsp fresh rosemary

Salt and pepper to taste

In a large 8 quart stock pot on medium-high heat add vegan butter, olive oil and onion. Cook down for 5 minutes then add garlic, carrots and celery. Cook down for another 5 minutes then add tomato paste, vegan Worcestershire sauce, thyme and rosemary. Cook for another few minutes then add red wine and tomatoes. Add lentils and veggie broth, 1 cup at a time. Cook for 20 minutes on medium low heat. Add peas and carrots and continue to cook for another 10 minutes.

Mashed potatoes:

6 to 8 russet potatoes

2 Tbsp plant-based butter

Buttermilk (½ cup plant-based milk with 2 tsp of apple cider vinegar)

Salt and pepper to taste

Paprika and chives for garnish

Peel and cook potatoes as you would regular mashed potatoes until tender. Once the potatoes are drained add buttermilk salt and pepper to taste. And mash until smooth consistency.

In a large baking dish at lentil feeling and half a cup at a time add potatoes on top of shepherd's pie and spread evenly. Then add paprika and chives for garnish on top and baked in the oven for 20 to 30 minutes. Enjoy!!!

IRISH SODA BREAD

Easiest bread you will ever make!! I make this every year for St Patty's Day!! May the luck of the Irish be with you today!!

3 cups flour

2 tsp salt

2 Tbsp baking soda

2 tsp baking powder

1 ½ cup your favorite Irish beers

Add flour, salt, baking soda and baking powder to a medium-sized mixing bowl and whisk together until well combined, then add your beer. In a cast iron skillet add a little bit of evoo at the bottom. And while your oven is heating up to 350° place your pan in there before you add the bread. Wait 10 minutes then add your bread mixture and cook for 20 to 30 minutes. Enjoy!!!

CHRISTMAS STUFFED BUTTERNUT SQUASH

Because Christmas is all about the colors and the food so why not have both!!!

1 large butternut squash

1 can of chickpeas, rinsed and drained

1 bag of baby spinach

3 cups cooked quinoa

A handful of fresh sage and thyme

½ cup cranberries

1 onion, chopped

1 Tbsp garlic

2 Tbsp olive oil

½ cup white wine

Salt and pepper to taste

Three large strands of kitchen string

Cut your butternut squash in half and take out the seeds. place on a cookie sheet face down with olive oil salt and pepper and bake in 400° oven for 45 minutes. While butternut squash is baking take another Tbsp olive oil in a large sauté pan on medium-high heat and place onion and garlic and sauté until translucent. Then take your chickpeas and put them in the pan with sage and thyme. Cook down for another 5 minutes. Take white wine and deglaze the pan for 2 minutes. Then take chopped spinach and cranberries and add to the pan and continue to cook for another few minutes then add in your cooked quinoa salt and pepper to taste. When your butternut squash is cooled off take a spoon and take out part of The middle and set aside for another recipe. then take your stuffing and place in both sides of the butternut squash and carefully Place one half of the butternut squash on top of the other tie it together with kitchen string and place in the oven for another 10 to 15 minutes. Enjoy!!! Merry Christmas to you and your family!!

HOLIDAY GREEN BEAN CASSEROLE

Green bean casserole is probably my favorite dish to look forward to during the holidays!! So here's a homemade version for you and your family to enjoy!!

6 cups frozen or fresh green beans

Cooked and drained.

One 8 oz container of mushrooms, sliced

1 small onion, sliced

1 Tbsp garlic

1 can of coconut full fat milk

½ cup plant based milk

1/8 cup soy sauce

3 Tbsp flour

2 Tbsp plant-based butter

2 Tbsp olive oil

1 canister of French's fried onions

Salt and pepper to taste

Start a saucepan on medium-high heat and add butter and olive oil and onion. Cook until starting to caramelize then add mushrooms. Once mushrooms have shrunk half in size add garlic and soy sauce and cook a few minutes more. Add flour and cook down for 1 minute then slowly whisk in coconut milk and almond milk. Once everything thickens like a gravy turn off heat and add salt and pepper to taste. Place cooked green beans in a large bowl then add the cream of mushroom soup mixture and mix until well combined. Place in 8"x 13" casserole dish and add French's fried onions on top. Bake in a 350° oven for 35 minutes!! Enjoy!!

THANKSGIVING TOFURKY

All right y'all I've been promising my tofurky recipe and here it is!! Happy Thanksgiving!!

Tofurky:

1 can of chickpeas rinsed and drained

1 pkg of extra firm tofu pressed for 30 minutes

4 cloves of garlic

¼ cup soy sauce

1 tsp garlic powder

1 tsp onion powder

1 tsp poultry seasoning

½ cup nutritional yeast

A handful of fresh sage

2 sprigs of fresh rosemary

1 tsp fresh thyme

1 cup veggie broth

2 cups vital wheat gluten

Glaze:

¼ cup maple syrup

1/8 cup balsamic vinegar

1/8 cup soy sauce

1 tsp garlic powder

1 tsp onion powder

Mix all ingredients in a small bowl and set aside. Combine all ingredients except for vital wheat gluten to a food processor, blend until smooth. I used my stand-up KitchenAid mixer for this but if you do not have one you can always do it by hand. Put your two cups vital wheat gluten in the mixing bowl as well as the ingredients from the food processor and using a dough hook place on setting number 2 for 5 to 10 minutes until combined and stretchy, the texture reminded me of

Play-Doh. Take it out of the mixing bowl and cut off two small balls. Place the rest on the counter and stretch it out like pizza dough. take a small bowl and place the dough inside the bowl stretched out over the sides. Then take your homemade stuffing and place inside the tofurky. Take the ends of your dough and stretch it back over the stuffing (recipe below) and close up dough around stuffing. Flip the bowl over onto a large piece of parchment paper and wrap the tofurky. Then place on a large piece of tin foil in again wrap up. Take the two small balls of dough from earlier and form into little drumsticks and do the same with them wrapped them in parchment paper and tin foil place on a baking sheet on 400 ° for 45 minutes to 1 hour. Then take out of the oven and mixed together ingredients for glaze brush the glaze on the tofurky and place back in the oven for another 15 minutes. The turkey should be nice and brown on top. Happy thanksgiving!!

THANKSGIVING MUSHROOM STUFFING

You can't have thanksgiving without the stuffing, and you can't make stuffing without old bread. My mom would always go down to Little Debbie's and ask for their day-old bread. I like using a good old fashioned French bread.

1 loaf of old crusty French bread diced

1 bushel of baby Bella mushrooms

3 stalks of celery, chopped

2 carrots, chopped

1 onion, chopped

4 cloves of garlic, minced

2-8 oz jars of veggie broth

1 cup white wine

1 Tbsp Dijon mustard

1 loaf of Italian bread

2 Tbsp fresh sage

2 Tbsp fresh thyme

2 Tbsp fresh rosemary

Salt and pepper to taste

Start off by dicing up the bread and placing it on a cookie sheet and in the oven at 400° for 10 minutes to get it nice and crunchy. In a cold pan start to sauté onions on low heat for 20 minutes until caramelized. When onions are nice golden brown color and tender add carrots and celery and garlic. Add mushrooms and cook down for 5 minutes. Deglaze with white wine and a little bit of veggie broth. Add a Tbsp Dijon mustard, thyme, rosemary, sage, salt and pepper to taste. Add the rest of the veggie broth and sauté for a few minutes longer. Take the bread out of the oven and place in a large bowl. Add the ingredients from your pan and mix together thoroughly place in an 8 by 8 casserole dish and in a 350° oven for 20 to 30 minutes!! Enjoy!!

THANKSGIVING MUSHROOM GRAVY AND GARLIC MASHED POTATOES

I'm a potato girl, you cannot get me away from them when they are around, but then, add gravy to it and I'm officially no longer available for the rest of the day!!

8 russet potatoes, peeled and diced

½ cup veggie broth

½ cup plant-based milk

1 bulb of garlic

Olive oil

Salt and pepper to taste

Gravy:

1 lb. of mushrooms

1 Tbsp vegan Worcestershire sauce

1 small onion, chopped

1 Tbsp plant-based butter

1 Tbsp thyme

½ cup white wine

¼ cup flour

8 oz veggie broth

Peel and dice potatoes, and place in cold water on stove and bring to boil. Potatoes are ready when fork tender, drain and set aside. Take bulb of garlic and slice the top of it off add olive oil, salt and pepper to taste and wrap up in tinfoil and place in 400° oven for 20 minutes. Let cool and squeeze cloves of garlic into mashed potatoes and add veggie broth and milk and more salt and pepper to taste. Beat with a hand beater for 10 minutes until smooth.

Gravy:

Add onion and butter to a cold sauté pan and bring up to high heat. Let onions caramelize for 20 minutes. Add mushrooms and continue to cook down for 10 more minutes. Add vegan Worcestershire sauce and cook a few minutes more. Add white wine and thyme and cook a few minutes more. Add flour and cook 5 minutes more than add veggie broth and whisk together until combined. Add salt and pepper to taste and serve. Enjoy!!

HOME-MADE CRANBERRY SAUCE

This is one of my favorite things to do at Thanksgiving!! I can't stand the canned crap, so when I found out how to make it myself I've never gone back.

- 1 bushel of cranberries

- 2 cinnamon sticks

- 1 tsp nutmeg

- 1 cup maple syrup

- 2 oranges (plus the peeling of one)

In a medium size saucepan add cranberries, cinnamon sticks, maple syrup, nutmeg and the juice of both oranges as well as the peeling of one. Simmer for 20 to 30 minutes then remove oranges and cinnamon sticks. Serve in a small bowl immediately or place in 8oz mason jars and refrigerate for up to 2 weeks. Enjoy!!

APPLE CIDER HOME-MADE

November is one of my favorite months!! Not just because the holidays are around the corner but also because it's my birthday month!! And I am so in love with holiday spices!! I went to Penzey's yesterday and stocked up on all kinds of new spices that I hadn't tried before!!! I ran into a small jar of mulling spices, and I had a bag of apples at home that needed to be eaten up immediately, so decided to make my own apple cider!!!

1 bag of Johnson apples roughly chopped no need to peel or core

2 cups maple syrup

2 Tbsp mulling spices

1 Tbsp cinnamon

16 cups water

You can cook this on the stove top for 8 to 12 hours on, but I threw all of the ingredients in the Instapot for 15 minutes and left it overnight. Best enjoyed on cool evenings next to a fireplace!!!

VEGAN VALENTINE'S DAY CUPCAKES!!

Batter:

- 4 ripe bananas
- 2 cups flour
- ½ cup sugar
- The juice of one lemon
- ½ cup plant-based milk
- 1 tsp baking soda
- 1 tsp baking powder
- 1 tsp cinnamon
- 1 tsp vanilla extract
- 2 Tbsp cocoa powder

Frosting:

- 2 sticks plant-based butter, room temperature
- 3 cups powdered sugar
- 4 Tbsp maraschino cherry juice

In a large bowl place bananas and mash them well. Add sugar and whisk until combined then add plant-based milk, vanilla extract, lemon juice and mix again. Add the remaining ingredients and mix until well combined. Scoop into individual muffin tins and bake in a 350° oven for 30 minutes.

For the frosting, in another bowl whisk butter with powdered sugar and maraschino cherry juice until well combined. When cupcakes are cooled, frost and sprinkle with sprinkles!! Enjoy!!!

NANA'S DATE BARS

My Nana and I used to bake in the kitchen together all the time. Growing up and these were my favorite thing to eat when I came to visit. Nana's 1930's Date bars made Vegan!!

For cookie crumble:

1 and 1/2 cups of oats

1 and 1/2 cups of flour

1 tsp of baking soda

1 cup of brown sugar

Two sticks of vegan butter

Melted

For the filling:

2 cups of chopped dates

1 cup of water

1/2 cup of sugar in the raw

In a medium sized bowl add your oats, flour, sugar, and baking soda and mix until well combined. Then add your melted vegan butter and mix again until it resembles oatmeal.

In a saucepan add your dates water and sugar and on medium high heat cook down for about 30 minutes until it's a thick paste.

In a 9x13 pan add half of your cookie mix and press until evenly spread. Then add your date mixture and spread evenly once again. Then crumble the rest of your cookie mixture on top. Bake the oven at 350° for 30 minutes. Enjoy!!

HARRY POTTER BUTTERBEER

Nothing says Harry Potter marathon like butterbeer!! I can finally say that I have a recipe that is very similar to the one that they serve down at universal. and I'm happy to say I've been able to make it vegan as well!!

For the marshmallow fluff:

Fourth of a cup of water

3/4 of a cup of sugar

Half a cup of maple syrup

One stick of vegan butter

1 tsp of vanilla extract

1 tsp of rum extract

One teaspoon of salt

2/3 of a cup of aquafaba juice from the can

1/4 of a teaspoon of cream of tartar

In a KitchenAid mixer with your whisk attachment add your aquafaba juice and cream of tartar and turn on high for about 3 to 5 minutes until stiff peaks appear like egg whites. In a medium sized saucepan add the rest of your ingredients to the pan on high heat. Add your candy thermometer and heat until 240° or softball state.

Then turn your KitchenAid mixer back on high and slowly add the butterscotch to the aquafaba mixture. Keep whisking on high for 10 to 12 minutes. Then place in an 8oz mason jar and refrigerate overnight. Mixture will become thicker with time.

For butterbeer:

One can of coconut milk full fat

1 tsp of vanilla extract

1 tsp of rum extract

For 12 oz bottles of cream soda

For better consistency place the coconut milk in fridge overnight so you can scrape off the fat from on top easier. Place the top part of coconut milk in a medium sized bowl leave the water use for smoothies later if you want.

Then whip the coconut milk for about 5 minutes then add your vanilla extract and rum extract and half of your butterscotch recipe that you made the day before.

Continue whipping until thick consistency. Then place one large spoonful at the bottom of a mug or butterbeer glass. And add your cream soda on top stir to combine and enjoy!!

PUMPKIN SPICE POUND CAKE FOR PRESCOTT

October is pregnancy and infant loss month. I had an experience of being able to be there for a sweet friend and her family after her daughter was stillborn. It was probably the most heartbreaking memory I have ever had to be a part of. I feel for all mothers who have gone through this and I pray for them every day. Holding a baby with no life truly changes you as a person. If you would like to donate to an organization that helps out with parents who deal with this, https://www.cuddlingangels.com/ is an

organization that helps provide incubator beds for children who are still born so the parents can mourn over them longer.

This is my recipe for little Prescott's birthday, She would have been 4 October 7th, 2020.

Fly high little angel!!

    Two sticks of vegan butter

    One cup of sugar in the raw

    Two and a half cups of flour

    1/4 of a cup of pumpkin puree

    1 tbsp of baking powder

    One teaspoon of salt

One teaspoon of cinnamon

Half a teaspoon of ginger

1/4 of a teaspoon of nutmeg

1/8 of a teaspoon of cloves

One cup of nut milk

1 tbsp of apple cider vinegar

For glaze:

One cup of powdered sugar

One teaspoon of almond extract

1 tsp of cinnamon

1 tbsp or two of nut milk

in a small bowl add your nut milk and your apple cider vinegar and place in the microwave for one minute to make buttermilk. in your KitchenAid stand up mixer add room temperature butter and sugar and mix until well combined.

Then add your buttermilk and your pumpkin puree and mix again.

Add your dry ingredients in a separate bowl and mix until well combined and slowly add to your wet ingredients.

Pour into a Bundt cake pan evenly coated with spray and Bake in a 350° oven for 40 minutes. On the side place all of your ingredients for your glaze and a small bowl and mix until well combined. Once the cake is cooled slowly tip it upside down on a plate and add your glaze and sprinkles if desired. Enjoy!!

CPSIA information can be obtained
at www.ICGtesting.com
Printed in the USA
LVHW071115220222
711715LV00015B/809

9 781525 592027